Praise for *Remaining with Jesus*

This is a wonderful work by a brilliant and deeply reflective Catholic writer. It is at one and the same time profound and accessible.

—Mark E. Thibodeaux, SJ

Remaining with Jesus

Discipleship in the Gospel of John

FATHER S. BRICE HIGGINBOTHAM

LOYOLAPRESS.
A JESUIT MINISTRY
Chicago

LOYOLAPRESS.

A JESUIT MINISTRY

www.loyolapress.com

Imprimatur:
Very Reverend Patrick J. Madden
Diocesan Administrator
Diocese of Houma-Thibodaux
16 July 2022

Cover art credit: javi.ruiz/iStock/Getty Images, M-image/iStockphoto/Getty Images, Miodrag Kitanovic/iStockphoto/Getty Images, YuliaBuchatskaya/iStock/Getty Images.

Back cover author photo, Mary Baird at Three Otters Photogaphy.

Special thanks to Rockridge Press for permission to reprint from *Daily Lessons from the Saints: 52 Weeks of Inspiration and Encouragement.*

ISBN: 978-0-8294-5459-8
Library of Congress Control Number: 2022945646

Printed in the United States of America.
22 23 24 25 26 27 28 29 30 31 Versa 10 9 8 7 6 5 4 3 2 1

To Mr. Todd Richard,
who first inspired in me a love for the Sacred Page;

Fr. Cassian Elkins, OSB,
who taught me how to receive spiritual nourishment from
this Word;

and to Dr. Brant Pitre, PhD,
who witnessed to me the integration of a deep technical
knowledge of historical criticism, a profound faith,
and abiding holiness.

Contents

Part 1

Introduction

1

Discipleship in the Bible

This book is about discipleship—in particular, the picture of discipleship the Holy Spirit reveals to us in the Gospel according to John. In these pages, you will find the fourth Gospel's answer to these questions: What does it mean to be a disciple of Jesus? How can we apply this knowledge to our own lives? How do we live as true disciples of the Lord? And finally, how do we know that we're doing so?

There are few more intimidating goals than reaching for true discipleship. *Who am I,* you might be asking yourself, *to think I can aspire to walk side by side with Jesus?* One of the purposes of this book is to unpack the many ways Scripture suggests that this is exactly what our aspirations should be. The second purpose of this book is to unveil clear and practical ways to apply the New Testament teachings of the Lord so that, just like His earliest disciples, you, too, can journey with Jesus.

As we journey together, our road map is simple. First, we will briefly study the etymology and context of key words related to discipleship. Then, we will quickly turn our attention to the Gospel of John and proceed step-by-step through the narrative in the order that John set down his thoughts. We will see that these teachings can be summarized in a four-part program of discipleship, the core of which is believing and remaining in Jesus: first, someone gives *witness to* us about Jesus; second, we come to *believe* in Him ourselves; third, we *remain* with Jesus and He with us; and fourth, we give evidence of our discipleship by showing the *love* of Jesus to one another.

Unveiling the Scriptural essence of this concept of discipleship begins with, no surprise here, *words.* The key is to track down the subtle shadings of the pertinent Greek and Hebrew words *within their context* because this is how we get to the root of their intentional meanings. This is where my personal search began, and it is my privilege to share what I learned about discipleship with you.

The Old Testament

In the Old Testament, I found much less than I expected. There are times when a person lives as a disciple or student of some teacher or master, but these times are relatively few and much less central than they are in the Gospels. The Old Testament uses the usual Hebrew word for disciple (*talmîd*) one time and the other word for disciple (*limmûd*) four times.[1] Discipleship did become important for the Jewish rabbis who were descended from the Pharisees of the New Testament period, but not until the second century after Christ. There are also other relationships in the Old Testament of masters and disciples in relationship with one another, but none of these scattered Old Testament prefigurations of discipleship captures the clear and consistent concept of discipleship that we see in the Gospels. Our search for the biblical understanding of discipleship, therefore, will be rooted in the New Testament.

1. John P. Meier, *A Marginal Jew: Rethinking the Historical Jesus,* vol. 3, *Companions and Competitors* (New Haven, London: Yale University Press, 2001), 42. The single use is merely to describe an apprentice musician in 1 Chronicles 25:8.

The New Testament

While the word *disciple* (Gk. *mathētēs*) is used 261 times in the New Testament, it is found only in the Gospels and in the Acts of the Apostles (the sequel to Luke's Gospel). It occurs exactly zero times in the remainder of the New Testament. Therefore, the only sections of the Scriptures in which the Greek word for disciple is used in a way relevant to our study are the Gospels and Acts.[2]

The substantial presence of the word *disciple* in just these books suggests that the concept of discipleship is of great importance for Jesus and the evangelists, and that it has some particular connection with the historical ministry of Jesus that, of course, overflows into the ministry of the Church. But what exactly was meant by this word *disciple* and, more important, this concept of discipleship? The words of Bible scholar Father John Meier are helpful:

> As we begin our quest for an adequate definition, we need to remind ourselves that the religious rhetoric of modern Christianity often leads us to use the word "disciple" quite loosely. The drive to be relevant pushes pulpit oratory and theological musings to employ the word "disciple" in as many meanings or in as broad a sense as possible . . . Perhaps some might prefer to stick with their intuition. They would simply take for granted that, since the basic meaning of *mathētēs* is "learner" or "student," a disciple of Jesus was anyone who listened to and learned the teachings of rabbi Jesus as one of his students. But the Gospels' picture of Jesus' disciples is not so simple.[3]

---

2. While it stands to reason that the New Testament concept of discipleship is informed by its Old Testament antecedents mentioned above, the vast usage of the concept and its circumscription into the single term μαθητής (*mathētēs*, "disciple") within the Jesus movement indicates the centrality of the concept of discipleship for Jesus and His followers beyond the emphasis given to it in its Old Testament antecedents.

3. *A Marginal Jew*, 3:49–50.

78 times

Father Meier deduces that the *absolute absence* of the term *disciple* in the letters of Paul, the Catholic Epistles, and Revelation, along with the fact that it does not figure prominently in the writings of other early Christians, indicate that the term was historically used by Jesus and His disciples. In other words, the word *disciple* was actually used in the time of Jesus and not just written into the Gospels because it was being used in the early church.[4]

Each time the word *disciple* is used in the Gospel according to John, it is clear that in the time of Jesus, the wider public was familiar with the word. The word *disciple* was used to describe a person with some association to a public figure. For example, when Jesus was on trial before Annas the high priest and Peter denied Jesus, multiple servants as well as Annas himself make reference to disciples of Jesus (John 18:16, 19, 25). This means either that the concept of discipleship was a common enough phenomenon in first-century Palestine that it was part of the normal language of the people, or that Jesus was particularly associated with disciples.[5]

The next question to answer is: Why focus on John? The answer is simple: Of the four Gospel accounts, John uses the word *disciple* more than any other: a total of seventy-eight times. Discipleship plays a more prominent role in the Gospel according to John than in any other book of the Bible. *believe remain*

The Gospel according to John

In the Gospel according to John, we find two key words for John's portrait of discipleship: *believe* and *remain*. He makes this especially

---

4. Meier, *A Marginal Jew*, 3:41.

5. See Meier, *A Marginal Jew*, 3:40–73. The Gospel according to John thrice mentions disciples of John the Baptist (John 1:35, 37; 3:25), and the Pharisees once refer to themselves as disciples of Moses (John 9:28). The Pharisees also had disciples, but these "disciples of the Pharisees" are mentioned in only two parallel passages, Mark 2:18 and Luke 5:33. Disciples of the Pharisees are not mentioned in John.

clear in John 8:31, where "Jesus said to the Jews who had believed [pisteúō] in him, 'If you remain [menō] in my word, you are truly my disciples [mathētēs].'"[6] A true disciple chooses to believe in Jesus, and this belief remains or abides through every struggle, always progressing toward a deeper faith. This doesn't mean that the true disciple never struggles or never stumbles but that he chooses Jesus again and again.[7]

Bible scholar Craig S. Keener writes, "Frequently John mentions that many 'believed' in Jesus (2:23; 7:31; 10:42; 11:45; 12:11, 42), but at least in many of these cases this faith proves inadequate to persevere for salvation."[8] The main takeaway here is that true discipleship requires both believing and remaining in Jesus. It's not enough for you and me to just believe that Jesus exists or that He works miracles. No; the deep joy promised by Jesus is for those disciples who come into relationship with Jesus and stay in relationship with Him—even through struggles, persecutions, and the repentance that is necessary when we fall short.

The Gospel presents real stories of real people who had real encounters with Jesus Christ and subsequently became His disciples. As we walk through the stories of those early disciples who believed and remained, we will encounter and explore what John presents as criteria for being a disciple of Jesus—namely believing (pisteúō) and remaining (menō). These experiences of the first disciples show us how we ourselves can live that kind of discipleship.

---

6. RSV-2CE translation adjusted by the author, based upon the Greek text (NA28).
7. Michael J. Wilkins, "Disciples and Discipleship," in *Dictionary of Jesus and the Gospels*, 2nd ed, ed. Joel B. Green, Jeannine K. Brown, and Nicholas Perrin (Downers Grove, IL: IVP Academic, 2013), 211.
8. Craig S. Keener, *The Gospel of John: A Commentary*, vol. 1 (Grand Rapids, MI: Baker Academic, 2003), 746. See also pp. 276–79.

Dynamics of Discipleship

Anchored by believing and remaining, there are four basic movements
by which a person becomes and lives as a disciple of Jesus. First, the
disciple begins to believe through some form of witness. The forms
of witness include but are not limited to a prophetic sign, the word
of another, the Scriptures, and inspiration from the Father. She then
encounters Jesus in a personal way, either physically, as during Jesus'
earthly life, or after His Ascension into heaven, through the Spirit
at work in the world. This personal encounter grounds and solidifies the disciple's belief. Then, empowered by Jesus, the new disciple
must choose to remain with Him, particularly through the suffering
which inevitably comes (John 15:5; 9:34–38; 16:33). This is a mutual
remaining that changes the focus of the disciple's life. Now her first
priority is her relationship with Jesus (John 6:56–57; 15:5). The disciple lives and acts not from her own power but from the power of
Jesus, with the Father and the Spirit (John 14:1–3, 16–17; 15). Her
true discipleship bears the fruit of practical love, which has the effect
of building up the Church and witnessing to other potential believers (John 8:31; 13:34–35; 15:16–17). Said another way, the basic
dynamic of each person's growth in discipleship goes something like
this, with believing and remaining in Jesus at the core of our journey:

1. I begin to **believe** because someone gives witness to me. In other
   words, someone tells me who Jesus is and how a relationship
   with Him makes a practical difference in his own life.

2. I have a **personal encounter** with Jesus, which solidifies that
   belief. I literally meet Jesus. As He walked upon the earth, people met Him physically. Now, we meet Him through the Holy
   Spirit whom He has sent. We encounter Him as we pray, in our
   neighbor, as we read the Scriptures, and especially in the
   Eucharist.

3. I choose to **remain** with Jesus, even through trials, temptations, and sufferings. I don't stop praying, reading Scripture, or receiving the sacraments, even when I encounter doubt, discouragement, or persecutions from others. If I fall into mortal sin, I go immediately to Reconciliation. I grow closer to the Father, Son, and Holy Spirit, sometimes in ways I can perceive and sometimes in ways that I can't perceive in the moment.

4. Empowered by the Holy Spirit, my believing and remaining bear fruit in practical *love* that builds up the Church and witnesses to other potential believers. I use the gifts that God has given me to help my fellow disciples live in closer and closer relationship with Jesus, and I share my faith with those who are not disciples. I help the poor. I tell others who Jesus is and how a relationship with Him makes a practical difference in my own life.

All four of these movements are essential to discipleship but believing and remaining are the two hinge actions that make the rest possible. In fact, we will come to learn that remaining is the natural consequence and perfection of a person's progress in faith/believing.

A Word about Language

The Gospel according to John (and the entire New Testament) was handed down to us in Greek. The Old Testament was written mostly in Hebrew, with some Greek and a little Aramaic. Reading our Bibles in English (a language that didn't even exist at the time of the New Testament) two thousand years after the biblical texts were written means that some things are literally lost in translation. As we discover what the Holy Spirit inspired St. John to write concerning discipleship, it is important for us to pay attention to the actual words St. John selected. Specific words aren't the only way an author communicates meaning—he also uses actions and context—but the words themselves are an important indication of the author's intention.

The Greek verb for "believe" is *pisteúō*. However, *pisteúō* can also mean "trust" in the sense of "to entrust oneself to an entity in complete confidence" or "entrust" as in "I entrust this precious family heirloom to you so that you might keep it safe." It can also mean "be confident about" or "think/consider possible." The nominal (noun) form of this word is *pístis*, commonly translated into English as "faith" or "belief," but sometimes meaning "trust, confidence, a pledge, or a commitment."[9] As we read our English Bibles, it is easy to miss some of the nuance of the Bible's meaning because using different English words unintentionally hides the fact that these concepts are expressed by the same word in Greek and are therefore very closely connected.

For "remain," we have a similar problem. The Greek verb *ménō* can be translated "remain, stay, abide, live, persist," and the like. The noun form is *mónē*, which in John means "a state of remaining in an area, staying, tarrying" or "a place where one stays, dwelling(-place), room, abode."[10] With these variations in language, even the most attentive reader of the Gospel in English will miss the connection between John 1:38, where Andrew and the other disciple ask Jesus, "Where do you live [*ménō*]?" and John 14:2, where Jesus tells us, "In my Father's house are many rooms [*mónē*]; if it were not so, would I have told you that I go to prepare a place for you?"

The fact is that these are different forms of the same word. At the beginning of the Gospel, Jesus' first disciples express their sprouting desire to live/remain with Jesus and, near the end of the Gospel, Jesus

---

9. See F. W. Danker, ed., *A Greek-English Lexicon of the New Testament and Other Early Christian Literature*, 3rd ed. (Chicago, IL: University of Chicago Press, 2000), 816–20, henceforth cited as BDAG.
10. See BDAG, 630–31, 658.

reveals that He has had a place prepared this whole time where He wants His disciples to live/remain with Him. This is the point of the whole Gospel, from beginning to end: Jesus comes to make true disciples who, having believed in Him, remain in the Heavenly communion that He shares with the Father and the Holy Spirit. It was only by reading John 14 in the original Greek that I myself was able to see this connection for the first time.

Getting the Most out of *Remaining with Jesus*

This book is set up to help us live our own discipleship. And discipleship only happens in relationship, first with Jesus, then almost always with fellow Christians here on earth. Every chapter ends with (1) a prayer to bring to Jesus what we've learned and ask Him for the help we need to live it; and (2) questions to discuss in small-group Bible study. You can meet once per week. You can meet once per month. You can meet in person or virtually. However you do it, the best way to live what you are learning is to come together with fellow disciples so that you can help one another in your journeys. If it isn't possible for you to get together with others, at least take some time to think about the questions on your own—maybe this can be part of your prayer time. Please do spend time writing down at least some of your answers. There's something about writing that makes things stick in our minds and hearts. Don't skip the prayer; actually pray it. And don't skip the questions; let Jesus speak to your heart through the words of His Gospel. Finally, if you're up for leading a small group but have questions about how to do it, turn to pages 87–88 for some tips.

Now that we know the basics, let's dive in to the first encounter between Jesus and His disciples. But first, I invite you to take a moment to pray. If you decide to pray these prayers with your Bible study group, change *I* to *we*, *me* to *us*, and *my* to *our*.

Let us pray: *Lord Jesus, You have called me to be Your disciple and have given me many examples to imitate. Aided by the prayers of the holy men and women whom I will meet in the pages of this book, give me the gift of faith, that I might believe in You, and the gift of courage, that I might remain with You. May I encounter You today. Teach me, dear Jesus, how to love my neighbor as myself for love of You. Amen.*

GOING DEEPER

Answers or possible answers are found on pages 89–90. But ponder the questions for yourself or share with your Bible study group before giving the answers a look.

- Where do you find yourself as we begin our journey together? What do you want out of this Bible study? What do you think when you hear the word *disciple* right now?

- In which books of the New Testament is the word *disciple* used? In which book does the word *disciple* appear most frequently? According to this chapter, what does this tell us about the use of the word *disciple* in the time of Jesus?

Read John 8:31; then discuss these questions in your group or ponder them on your own.

- According to John 8:31, what are the two central things that a true disciple does? What do you think when you hear the word *believe* right now? The word *remain*?

- According to pages 8–9 above, what are the four basic dynamics of a person's growth in discipleship? How does this describe your experience of discipleship?

- What are you most excited about as we begin to learn about discipleship together? How can the people in your Bible study (or your other friends) pray for you?

Part 2

The First Disciples

2

The Disciples Meet Jesus |
John 1

When did you meet Jesus? What made you decide to follow Him? Our stories are full of conversions. Some of us have experienced big, dramatic conversions. Others, like me, have quiet little conversions over and over again. Having a conversion just means that I turn toward Jesus. But some conversions are bigger than others, and sometimes we have to take big steps in order to follow after Him. In this chapter, we'll walk with Jesus' first followers as they take their first big steps as disciples.

Andrew, the Other Disciple, and Simon Peter | John 1:29–42

Near the very beginning of St. John's Gospel, we meet Jesus' first disciples: Andrew; an unnamed disciple often thought to be John himself; Peter; Philip; and Nathanael.[11] Andrew and the unnamed

---

11. See Rudolf Bultmann, *The Gospel of John: A Commentary*, trans. G. R. Beasley-Murray (Oxford: Basil Blackwell, 1971), 108; Raymond E. Brown, *The Gospel according to John, I—XII*, Anchor Yale Bible series, vol. 29 (New Haven, CT:, 1966), 73, (who later changes his position in *An Introduction to the Gospel of John*); and Craig S. Keener, *The Gospel of John: A Commentary*, 468. However, even in the aforementioned works, knowledge of the other disciple's identity is in no way conclusive.

disciple start out as disciples of John the Baptist and, believing the Baptist's witness, begin to remain with Jesus:

> [John] saw Jesus coming toward him, and said, "Behold, the Lamb of God, who takes away the sin of the world. . . . And I have seen and have borne witness that this is the Son of God." The next day again John was standing with two of his disciples; and he looked at Jesus as he walked, and said, "Behold, the Lamb of God!" The two disciples heard him say this, and they followed Jesus. (John 1:29, 34–37)

Believing the witness of their teacher, these two disciples follow Jesus, who initiates a conversation with them: "What [or, whom] do you seek?" (John 1:38a).[12] The disciples respond in a way both simple and profound. "Rabbi" (which means Teacher), "where are you staying [*remaining*]?" (John 1:38b). What do the disciples mean when they ask this question? Are they just asking for Jesus' address, or are they searching for something more? Certainly, Andrew and the other disciple want to be in Jesus' physical presence; they want to follow Him and learn from Him. But they also want something more. True disciples want to know where Jesus remains because they want to be with Him and remain there themselves. As Andrew and the other disciple follow Jesus, He turns to them and asks the same question that He will ask Mary Magdalene after the Resurrection, indeed the

---

12. "This now is the 'First Word' of Jesus in the Gospel of John. And in this case the First Word is a First Question. Jesus asked them, 'What are you seeking?' (1:38). A variant reading stands in some ancient manuscripts: 'Whom are you seeking?' One of the things that makes me pounce on this as a significant utterance is the fact that close to the end of this same Gospel, Jesus asks almost the same question. At the tomb on Easter morning, Jesus puts a question to Mary Magdalene, who has still not recognized him and who is still weeping despite finding the tomb empty and in spite of having been granted a vision of two angels, one sitting where His head had been and one where His feet had rested, Jesus asked her, 'Whom are you seeking?' Again, ancient texts offer a variant reading. This time the variant is, 'What are you seeking?' It is almost as though this question brackets the entire gospel." (Robert H. Smith, "Seeking Jesus in the Gospel of John," *Currents in Theology and Mission*, 15:1 (1988), 52).

same question He asks each of us who begin the walk of discipleship, "What [or, whom] do you seek?" (John 1:38b). Simply put, it is Jesus who calls. It is Jesus who invites. And His invitation implies more than a surface-level question about the walking habits of Andrew and the unnamed disciple. It is an invitation that speaks to the very heart of human beings: our desire to *be with God*.[13] As we recognize that walking in the ways of the world leaves us ever unsatisfied, Jesus invites us to walk after Him. He invites us to come and see something permanent, something beyond this world of limitations, change, and death. He invites us to come and see a place where we can remain forever.[14] Through our belief in Him, we will become children of God and, as children in the Son, can remain in the house of the Father forever.[15]

For their part, Andrew and the unnamed disciple did come, and they did see. Importantly, they began to remain with Jesus. Then, empowered by his remaining with Jesus, Andrew immediately bore fruit in his witness to his brother Simon Peter. Andrew finds Peter and brings him to Jesus. Having found such a treasure, Andrew cannot help but share the Good News.[16] If we take a step back and look at the trajectory of this story line, we see again the Gospel's four-part progression in discipleship. Andrew (1) believes the witness of John the Baptist, (2) has a personal encounter with Jesus, (3) remains with Jesus, (4) and bears fruit in the practical, loving action of bringing his brother to Jesus the Messiah. This process, however, wasn't just for Andrew's first meeting with Jesus. Being a disciple of Jesus

13. Brown, *The Gospel according to John I—XII*, 78–79.
14. See John 14:2.
15. See John 1:12, 8:35; 14:1–2; and John Paul II, "Homily for the Solemnity of Mary, Mother of God" (1 January 1997), http://www.vatican.va/content/john-paul-ii/en/homilies/1997/documents/hf_jp-ii_hom_19970101.html, 3.
16. John 1:39–42. The Greek word translated "gospel" is *euangélion*, which literally means "good news."

is a way of life in relationship with a person. Building habits and growing in relationships take time and effort, along with many stumbles, mistakes, doubts, and apologies along the way. We want to be like Andrew, but we have to remember that even Andrew wasn't like Andrew every day. Stay with Jesus. Witness to others. And when you fail—because we all fail sometimes—get up, repent, and keep moving forward.

The way that Andrew lived this process of growth in discipleship reminds me of someone I know. Allow me to share her story with you.

Several years ago, I met a young college athlete who was (and still is) like Andrew. In a way similar to how John the Baptist pointed Andrew toward Jesus, a holy missionary had been clearly and directly pointing this woman to Jesus. She had started remaining with Jesus by spending time in Eucharistic Adoration, by diving into the Scriptures, and by going to the sacraments as frequently as she could. She had always been the kind of girl who went to church, but something was different now; she had been invited into something more. Worldly fun was no longer going to rule her life. She decided that she wasn't going to drink alcohol (even in moderation) until the legal age. And she was going to do everything she could to introduce others to Jesus. She messed up from time to time. She fell back into her old ways on occasion. In fact, she was and still is in the process of discipleship. What changed was that now she would repent if ever she slid back into her old habits. She arrived at a place where, even though her old sins sometimes tripped her up, they no longer ruled her life. Soon, they began to fade away.

This young lady was one of the best to ever play her position in her sport at her university. She used her platform to gently and clearly tell people about Jesus so well that all over town I would hear about Megan, this amazing young lady who witnessed to Jesus with her words and by her life. After college, she devoted two years to introducing other people to Jesus on another college campus in another state, and now she spends her days inviting the high school students she teaches to come to know Him. Megan is doing today just what Andrew did two thousand years ago. She didn't wait until she had it all together to give witness. She didn't say, "I don't remain with Jesus 100 percent of the time, so I shouldn't even try." No. Even today, as she was sure to remind me when I asked if I could include her story in this book, she fails and sins. She considers that she is still in the process. Even so, she remains with Jesus in Adoration, in Scripture, and in the sacraments more often than not. When she doesn't, she repents, coming back into the embrace of Jesus.

What about you? What about me? Think about what it might look like to be Andrew or to be John the Baptist in your own way and in your own life, as we walk with the next two disciples who are shown to us in the Gospel.

Philip and Nathanael | John 1:43–51

The day after Jesus calls Andrew and the other disciple, Jesus calls Philip, who turns around and extends that same invitation to his friend Nathanael:

> The next day Jesus . . . found Philip and said to him, "Follow me." . . . Philip found Nathanael, and said to him, "We have found him of whom Moses in the law and also the prophets wrote, Jesus of Nazareth, the son of Joseph." Nathanael said to him, "Can anything good come out of Nazareth?" Philip said to him, "*Come and see.*" (John 1:43–46, emphasis added.)

Philip chooses to follow Jesus. That's good. Even better, he can't help but tell his friend Nathanael about Jesus. When Nathanael expresses doubt, Philip simply brings him to Jesus. The personal witness of other people opens us up to faith and begins to draw us into relationship. Remember Megan's story? Even though she was already the kind of girl who went to church, it was the personal invitation of a missionary who wanted to be her friend that led her to remain with Jesus and, in turn, lead others to Him.

But the invitation must give way to encounter. No amount of my telling you about my relationship with Jesus can make you experience it for yourself. Nathanael's story bears this out.

At first, Nathanael is skeptical. When Philip tells him that the Messiah whom he found comes from Nazareth, Nathanael responds disparagingly, "Can anything good come out of Nazareth?" (John 1:46a). As a good friend and wise missionary, Philip doesn't respond to Nathanael's doubt by trying to convince him. He simply says, "Come and see." (John 1:46b). Nathanael does come, and he does see. Jesus sees him coming as if He were waiting just to speak personally to Nathaniel. The Lord responds to his doubt in one sentence that makes all the difference, and Nathanael begins to believe. Before long, he is confessing that Jesus is the Son of God and the King of Israel. What Philip could not have achieved with a whole day of debate, Jesus accomplishes in a moment. Philip witnesses, Nathanael encounters Jesus, and there at the beginning of belief he begins to be a disciple.[17] Soon, Nathanael, along with the other disciples, will remain with Jesus and eventually will give his own witness. Over and over again, he will invite others to come and see.

"Come and See" | John 1:39, 46

How can we do today what Andrew and Philip did two thousand years ago? It starts with courage. It starts with action. Don't believe that telling others about Jesus is for someone else. This is not something that is just for the disciples of the past. Sharing in the joy of

---

17. See Craig S. Keener, *The Gospel of John*, 2 vols. (Grand Rapids, MI: Baker Academic, 2003), 472, 485.

witnessing to Jesus is for you and for me, disciples today! To do that, we first remain with Jesus in prayer, Scripture, and sacraments. There, Jesus allows me to experience His desire for personal relationship with me and moves me to begin to share His desire for relationship with others. Then, I share the fruits of my own relationship with Jesus and invite others to experience the same. We can see how to share those fruits from the examples of Philip and Andrew.

First, as we've already seen, neither Andrew nor Philip start with complicated arguments. Putting it into today's lingo, they say, "I've found what you've been looking for. Come; let me show you." Peter, Andrew's brother, and Nathanael, Philip's friend, were searching. And the point here may be that every human being is searching. We all want to fill the longing that persists in our hearts until we find what we were made for. "What were we made for?" you ask. We were made by God and for God—by Love, for Love. In other words, we were made in His image, and it is impossible to stamp that image out. So even if they only have the tiniest spark of a desire for God, invisible even to themselves, we start where our friends are. For example, Philip starts from where Nathanael is. Philip doesn't start from where Philip is, nor does he start from where he wants Nathanael to be. Nathanael was already interested in God's promises. He already knew that a Messiah would come to save us. God had already revealed this through Moses and the prophets. So Philip tells his friend, "We have found him of whom Moses in the law and also the prophets wrote, Jesus of Nazareth, the son of Joseph" (John 1:45). After starting where his friend is, Philip introduces something new, the person of Jesus the Messiah. Philip has introduced Nathanael to the fulfillment and completion of his search.

We, too, in witnessing to others, must proclaim the newness of relationship with Jesus Christ. But if we are going to be effective, we must show how Christ is the fulfillment of our friends' longing. Pope St. John Paul II pointed this out not so long ago:

> It is Jesus in fact that you seek when you dream of happiness; he is waiting for you when nothing else you find satisfies you; he is the beauty to which you are so attracted; it is he who provokes you with that thirst for fullness that will not let you settle for compromise; it is he who urges you to shed the masks of a false life; it is he who reads in your hearts your most genuine choices, the choices that others try to stifle. It is Jesus who stirs in you the desire to do something great with your lives, the will to follow an ideal, the refusal to allow yourselves to be ground down by mediocrity, the courage to commit yourselves humbly and patiently to improving yourselves and society, making the world more human and more fraternal.[18]

Because he loves the other person, the disciple begins where the other is and tries, by God's grace, to walk with her on the path to belief in Jesus. This is how disciples share Jesus with others.

Let us pray: *Lord Jesus, Your first disciples wanted to be near You more than anything else. Being near You, they also invited others into Your holy presence. Draw us near to You in joy, kind Master, and give us the skill and the courage to bear effective witness of Your love to all whom we encounter, especially our family and friends. Amen.*

---

18. John Paul II, Address at the Prayer Vigil for the Fifteenth World Youth Day, Rome, (August 19, 2000), http://w2.vatican.va/content/john-paul-ii/en/speeches/2000/jul-sep/documents/hf_jp-ii_spe_20000819_gmg-veglia.html.

GOING DEEPER

Answers or possible answers are found on pages 90–92. But ponder the questions for yourself or share with your Bible study before giving the answers a look.

- Where do you find yourself as a disciple today? Has anything changed since you started this book?

Read John 1:35–46; then discuss these questions in your group, or ponder them on your own.

- Who introduced you to Jesus? Who was your John the Baptist, Andrew, or Philip? How did they do it?
- What did Andrew and the other disciple do when they met Jesus? Why do you think this is important?
- What else did Andrew do as a result of meeting Jesus? Can you see yourself in Andrew's place in the story? What does that look like to you?
- What are the two steps of Nathanael's first encounter with Jesus? Why do you think each of these steps is important?
- In John 1, what is Jesus teaching us about discipleship?

Reread the quote from Pope St. John Paul II on page 77; then discuss or ponder on your own.

- What are some ways that our culture "dreams of happiness"? What are one or two hopes and desires of people in the world today that can be points of contact with the Gospel?

Remember Megan's story from pages 18–19:

- She remained with Jesus through Eucharistic Adoration, diving into the Scriptures, and approaching the sacraments. Does this sound like a life that you want to live?

What are some of the roadblocks to living this life? Which one of these three (Adoration, Scriptures, and sacraments) can you engage with this week? Who will help by keeping you accountable to making the effort to remain with Jesus?

- Megan used her platform as an athlete to share her faith. What platforms do you have? Who listens to you? Whom can you gently and clearly introduce to Jesus? And how will you make the introduction? Who will keep you accountable to actively witnessing your faith to others? **(Note:** Digital platforms are fine, but also think about more personal opportunities to gently and organically talk about Jesus.)

- After walking through the true story of the call of the first disciples, how do you feel? How can the other people in your Bible study (or your other friends) pray for you?

3

Discipleship Is a Process | John 2

In the second chapter of his Gospel, St. John tells us about Jesus' first big miracle, which he calls a sign. This miraculous sign is an early training ground for the disciples: will they have what's called "signs faith," which is a surface-level belief based upon miracles, excitement, and emotion? Or will they begin to believe in Jesus personally by placing their trust in Him? Jesus does not expect them to have total faith in Him yet—they've just met, after all! But He is inviting them past a faith based only on signs into the beginnings of true belief. Jesus says that His signs are an important starting point for faith, but they must lead to more.

The setting is a wedding reception in a village called Cana where the host ran out of wine. Jesus' mother, Mary, tells him about this problem and, since the coming of the Messiah was supposed to provide abundant wine for God's people, Jesus turns water into wine as the first of His signs. This is a sign that He is the Messiah sent from God to save His people.[19]

---

19. Brant Pitre, *Jesus the Bridegroom* (New York: Image, 2014), 38–42. See Amos 9:11, 13 and Joel 3:18.

Let's review the progression of the esteem Jesus was beginning to earn. First, Andrew told Peter that he had found the Messiah. Then Philip told Nathanael that this Jesus was the one of whom Moses and the prophets had written. Here at Cana, with this sign, Jesus is seen as the divine Messiah. The disciples become convinced about who Jesus is and what He promises.

Their experience shows us that discipleship is a process.

The Disciples Believe | John 2:1–11

In John 1, Andrew and the other disciple started out as disciples of John the Baptist, not of Jesus. Then, when John sent them to Jesus (because that was John's mission), they remained with Jesus only for an evening. In fact, none of the disciples whom we met in John 1 are called disciples of Jesus—not yet. They must get to know Him better. They must grow in relationship. They must believe in Him. This they begin to do when they see the water changed to wine:

> This, the first of his signs, Jesus did at Cana in Galilee, and manifested his glory; and his disciples believed [*pisteúō*] in him. (John 2:11)

As the Gospel progresses, we will see their belief deepen based upon their knowledge of the person of Jesus. Eventually, they will learn that the fullness of belief lies in remaining with Him, especially through suffering.

The Disciples Remain | John 2:12

The Gospel just told us that the disciples believed in Jesus, and in the very next sentence, it goes on to mention that they remained with Him:

After this he went down to Capernaum, with his mother and his brothers and his disciples; and there they remained [*ménō*] not many days. (John 2:12)[20]

This reminds us that disciples must never forget to remain with Jesus, and in fact, we must remain with Him more as our relationship deepens. We are meant to remain with Him not just physically and not only for hours or for days as the disciples did here, but forever—a truth that the first disciples will soon learn.

Belief without Remaining: The People of Jerusalem | John 2:23–25

A little later, Jesus and His disciples go up to Jerusalem where He performs another sign, the effect of which is to lead more people into belief. But the belief of the people here is different from the belief of the disciples:

> Now when he was in Jerusalem at the Passover feast, many believed [*pisteúō*] in his name when they saw the signs which he did; but Jesus did not trust [*pisteúō*] himself to them, because he knew all men and needed no one to bear witness of man; for he himself knew what was in man. (John 2:23–25)

The people in Jerusalem clearly have some faith, but the fact that Jesus did not trust Himself to them shows that something is lacking. Despite being impressed by Jesus' miracles, they were not open to relationship with Him.[21] The miracles that God sometimes works are meant to be a spark that ignites or strengthens our faith in Jesus, but this spark of faith is only the beginning of discipleship.

---

20. RSV-2CE translation adjusted by the author, based upon the Greek text (NA28).
21. Craig S. Keener, *The Gospel of John*, 2 vols. (Grand Rapids, MI: Baker Academic, 2003), 531. See also Rudolf Bultmann, *The Gospel of John: A Commentary*, trans. G. R. Beasley-Murray (Oxford, Basil Blackwell, 1971), 130–31.

How many people see God's hand at work in the moment of the healing of a loved one, either through a miracle or through medical care, only to return to their sins after the emotion wears off and the drama is resolved? How many of us have a powerful experience of God in prayer, either alone or during the liturgy at church, then return to our old patterns of sin? If we want to be true disciples of Jesus, we must root this faith in our souls by remaining with Jesus—by coming back into His presence repeatedly and receiving more deeply the graces that He fervently desires to bestow upon us. We do whatever we can to bear witness to Jesus—not just to the signs and wonders but also to the depths of discipleship, which is relationship with Him. This doesn't mean that we never sin or backslide. But it does mean that when we mess up, we repent, get back up, and continue the journey.

Liar, Lunatic, or Lord?

As we bring this chapter to a close, let's take a moment to talk about how we see Jesus today. Even today, many see Jesus as merely a great teacher or role model, like Gandhi, the Buddha, Confucius, or Nelson Mandela. But the Bible shows us that Jesus is God. The great Anglican apologist C. S. Lewis famously teaches that since Jesus claimed to be God, He cannot be merely a great teacher or excellent moral example. Jesus is either a liar (claiming to be God while knowing that He isn't), a lunatic (claiming to be God, believing that He was God, but actually not God) or Lord (truly God come in the flesh).[22] Lewis invites us to faith in the real Jesus, who is not *merely* a good

---

22. Recent atheists have added a fourth option—legend—claiming that the Gospels are later projections onto the life of Jesus, who never actually claimed to be God. But the Gospels are, in fact, very reliable historical documents in which are recorded the real words and deeds of Jesus, who really did claim to be God. For a clear and rather complete treatment of this see Brant Pitre, *The Case for Jesus: The Biblical and Historical Evidence for Christ* (New York: Image, 2016).

teacher, or *merely* a good moral example, or *merely* a miracle worker. Instead, we are invited to believe in Jesus the God-man who changes our lives.

Let us pray: *Jesus most gentle, teach us patience. May we be always patient with ourselves yet never patient with our sin. Recognizing our weakness, may we ever bow before You, God Almighty, humbly asking that You raise us when we stumble, strengthen us when we stand tall, and lead us always on the path of discipleship. Amen.*

GOING DEEPER

Answers or possible answers are found on pages 92–94. But ponder the questions for yourself, or share with your Bible study before giving the answers a look.

- Where do you find yourself as a disciple today? Has anything changed since you started this book?

Read John 2:1–11; then discuss these questions in your group, or ponder them on your own.

- What miracle did Jesus perform at the wedding in Cana? What did it signify? Especially in light of Philip's conversation with Nathanael explored in chapter 2 of this book, why do you think this particular miracle may be important?
- Do you believe in Jesus?
- If so, what were some of the first things that began to convince you? Was it the witness of another person? Was it a miracle, a big blessing, or a powerful emotional experience?
- If not, what are you looking for? What do you think might move you to both believe and work to remain?
- What new things have you learned about discipleship in John 2?

Read John 2:11–12 and 23–25; then discuss these questions in your group, or ponder them on your own.

- What's different between the disciples' response to Jesus and the response of the people in Jerusalem? Based upon your reading of this chapter, why might it be that their responses were different?

- The people in Jerusalem could not enter into a trusting relationship with Jesus. Are there places in your life where you struggle to trust Jesus? What or who might be able to help you trust Jesus more in one of these areas?

- Have you ever experienced a miracle? Have you ever experienced powerful emotional experiences with Jesus? What did you learn from those experiences? How did you (or did you not) allow the miracle(s) or the emotional experience(s) to lead you deeper into relationship with Jesus?

- After walking with the first disciples as they begin to grow in their discipleship, how do you feel? What's in your mind and heart regarding Jesus today? How can the other people in your Bible study (or your other friends) pray for you?

Part 3

The Path of Discipleship

4

Believe Like a Samaritan | John 4

In John 4, we meet a town of Samaritans who believe in Jesus through hearing, without the benefit of experiencing any physical signs. Then, even without a sign, they choose to invite Jesus to remain with them.

Who Are the Samaritans?

This stop on our journey to an understanding of discipleship takes us to the region of Samaria. To understand the importance of this scene, we need to ask, "What is Samaria?" and "Who are the Samaritans?"[23]

Samaria was part of the Promised Land that God gave to His people after freeing them from Egypt and leading them through the desert. Yet after the time of King Solomon, the land was split in two: the kingdom of Israel in the north (including the city of Samaria, which would become its capital) and the kingdom of Judah in the south (including the city of Jerusalem). This caused the beginning of a rivalry that lasted into the time of Jesus and beyond. To make matters worse, the kingdom of Israel and its capital city were conquered by the Assyrian Empire in 722 BC. Many residents were deported, and people who worshiped various false gods were brought

---

23. Scott Hahn, *Catholic Bible Dictionary* (New York: Doubleday, 2009), 805–8.

in to populate the region. These newcomers continued to worship their own gods even as they began to worship the God of Israel (2 Kings 17:26–28). According to the Old Testament books of Ezra and Nehemiah, even the native Samaritans who had not been carried into exile fell into this practice of breaking the first commandment by worshiping false gods alongside the one true God.

In Jesus' day, the region of Samaria was situated between the region of Galilee in the north (where Jesus spent much of His time) and Jerusalem in the south. When traveling from Galilee to Jerusalem, a Jew was faced with the choice of taking a shorter path through Samaria or a longer path around Samaria. So great was their hostility for each other that most Jews would take the longer path just to avoid traveling through Samaria. Jesus, however, took the short path in order to give the Samaritans an opportunity to become His disciples.[24] "In Jesus' teaching [and actions]," Bible scholar Scott Hahn writes, "the Samaritans were a powerful means of expressing the truly radical call he was making in the Gospel. . . . As there was in first-century Palestine no greater feud than that between the Samaritans and the Jews, Jesus made the stunning demand that love of neighbor meant loving the Samaritan, and brotherhood included such a bitter enemy."[25] This is striking! Jesus, having been rejected by some Jews and being a Jew Himself, scandalously reaches out to longtime rivals. The message is: anyone who is willing to believe and remain is welcome to become His disciple.

A Harvest of Disciples | John 4:39–42

With this background in mind, we see part of the beauty of Jesus' invitation to discipleship: it is not limited to a certain race or to a

24. Francis Martin and William M. Wright IV, *The Gospel of John* (*Catholic Commentary on Sacred Scripture*) (Grand Rapids, MI: Baker Academic, 2015), 81.
25. Hahn, *Dictionary*, 808.

privileged few but is extended even to those whom we might think are unworthy.[26] Jesus wants us to see the harvest of souls that can be won.

> [The Samaritan townspeople] went out of the city and were coming to him. . . . [And Jesus said to his disciples,] "Do you not say 'There are yet four months, then comes the harvest'? I tell you, lift up your eyes, and see how the fields are already white for harvest." (John 4:30, 35)

The harvest is the discipleship of the people of the Samaritan town Sychar.

> Many Samaritans from that city believed [*pisteúō*] in him because of the woman's witness, "He told me all that I ever did." So when the Samaritans came to him, they asked him to remain [*ménō*] with them; and he remained [*ménō*] there two days. And many more believed [*pisteúō*] because of his word. They said to the woman, "It is no longer because of your words that we believe [*pisteúō*], for we have heard for ourselves, and we know that this is indeed the Savior of the world" (John 4:39–42).[27]

As it happened with John the Baptist and the first disciples, so, too, the faith of the people of Sychar is prepared by a witness. Here, it is the woman who witnesses after her encounter with Jesus. The people of Sychar are willing to give Jesus a hearing on the basis of her word, but they must encounter Jesus Himself to widen, strengthen, and deepen their initial faith (John 4:42). In short, they must remain with Jesus. We see again the centrality of believing and remaining. But we also see the near necessity of someone giving witness to spur others into belief.

Because they now believe in Him, the Samaritans ask Jesus to remain with them, which leads to even more belief. But there's

---

26. See John 2:23–25; 5:9–47.
27. RSV-2CE translation adjusted by the author, based upon the Greek text (NA28).

something in the faith of the Samaritans that we haven't encountered before. These people believe without seeing the spectacle of physical signs. The disciples had believed in Jesus when they saw Him turn water into wine, which was good. But the Samaritans take it to the next level. Merely hearing the woman's witness about her own encounter with Jesus was enough for them to begin to believe. Thus, it seems that these Samaritans show an impressive depth of faith and receive in advance the blessing about which Jesus speaks near the end of the Gospel: "You have believed because you have seen me. Blessed are those who have not seen and yet believe" (John 20:29). By their believing and by Jesus' remaining with them, we see that the Samaritans of Sychar are true disciples of Jesus and models of discipleship for us.

The Woman at the Well | John 4:7–30

The Samaritans were introduced to Jesus by the witness of the "woman at the well." Who is this woman who brings her whole village onto the path of discipleship? An ancient tradition tells us that having been baptized, she took the name Photina and, dying for Christ as a martyr, became a saint.[28] Since she was part of the group of Samaritans who believed in Jesus and with whom He remained, she, too, is a true disciple. She is the protodisciple of the Samaritans. Therefore, let's look at St. Photina's encounter with Jesus to give us more insight into our own journey as His disciples.

I see six stages of increasing belief in Photina's first encounter with Jesus. Don't pain yourself looking for these six steps in your own life. You are unique and Photina is unique. But, since we're all humans, some parts of her journey will surely be helpful for you and for me.

---

28. Benedict XIV, *The Roman Martyrology* (Baltimore: John Murphy and Co., 1916), 81.

Stage 1: Upon meeting Jesus, the woman first recognizes only His ethnicity and the difference between them: "How is it that you, a Jew, ask a drink of me, a woman of Samaria?" (John 4:9)

Stage 2: When Jesus says that He can give her living water, she responds with the respectful title *sir* (Greek, *kýrios*), and asks if He thinks He is greater than her ancestor Jacob (John 4:11–12). This Greek word *kyrios* has multiple meanings, and the difference between them is important. *Kyrios* can be a simple, respectful greeting like the English "sir"; it can show honor to a person of significant status such as a king, or like the English "lord"; or it can be used to refer to God Himself, *Lord* with a capital *L*. For now, Photina is only using it to mean "sir."

Stage 3: Jesus takes it up a notch. He tells her that the person who drinks His water will never thirst. Astonishingly, she seems to believe Him: "Sir [*kýrios*], give me this water, that I may not thirst, nor come here to draw" (John 4:15). Now, it seems like her *kýrios* means more than just "sir." Is Jesus greater than her revered ancestor Jacob? If He can provide ever-satisfying water, He most certainly is! But being a great miracle worker who deserves the title *Lord* doesn't yet mean that He is the Messiah, and certainly doesn't yet mean that He is God.

Stage 4: But Jesus continues. He gives her a sign but not an external sign. He shows her that He knows her heart and cares about her life:

> Jesus said to her, "Go, call your husband, and come here." The woman answered him, "I have no husband." Jesus said to her, "You are right in saying, 'I have no husband'; for you have had five husbands, and he whom you now have is not your husband; this you said truly." The woman said to him, "Sir [*kýrios*], I perceive that you are a prophet" (John 4:16–19).

First, she saw Jesus as only another Jew. Then she addressed Him more politely. After that, she understood something of His power. In fact, she comes to see Him as a prophet and, more than a prophet, the Messiah Himself:[29]

> The woman said to him, "I know that Messiah is coming (he who is called Christ); when he comes, he will show us all things." Jesus said to her, "I who speak to you am he." (John 4:25–26)

Her faith has been progressing throughout this encounter with Jesus and now, with no external miracles, this plain, sinful person has come to believe in Jesus the Messiah even though she doesn't know Him completely or have it all figured out.

Stage 5: Changed by her encounter with Jesus, she goes forth to bear witness to this man who may be the Christ (John 4:28–29).[30] And when the others came to Christ, they also began to believe.

Stage 6: Finally, Jesus remains with Photina and her fellow Samaritans (John 4:40), who together believe in Jesus and remain with Him, thereby beginning their own journey of true discipleship.

St. Photina's growth in belief came quickly—from one conversation and two days in the village with Jesus—but it did not come all at once. It came in stages, and it came as she willingly engaged with Him. To live as disciples today, we, like St. Photina, must willingly engage with Him over and over again, and then also choose to give missionary witness to Jesus. Bottom line: discipleship is an ongoing missionary process. We must become missionary disciples.

---

29. Raymond E. Brown, *The Gospel according to John I—XII*, Anchor Yale Bible series, vol. 29 (New Haven, CT: Yale University Press, 1966), 170.

30. The word *Messiah* is the Hebrew word for "anointed one," which is translated into Greek as "Christ." They have the same meaning and are used interchangeably.

A Woman Disciple?

St. Photina is clearly a disciple of Jesus. But some people disagree. Some point out that this Samaritan woman is never explicitly called "disciple" in the Gospel. Moreover, only once in the whole Bible is a woman referred to as a disciple (Acts 9:36). Can a woman be a disciple? Of course! But then why wouldn't women be called disciples more often in the Bible?

While it is true that the word *disciple* is not used in the Gospel to describe St. Photina, it is equally true that Andrew, John, Peter, Philip, and Nathanael are not identified as disciples of Jesus in their first encounter with Him. It is only in the next scene, the wedding at Cana described in John 2, where they are identified as His disciples.

Just like Philip, Photina brought others to Jesus, but whereas Philip brought one person, Photina brought an *entire town*! She does the same thing as Philip, but by virtue of sheer numbers, she does more.[31] Therefore, not only must she qualify as a disciple, but perhaps she is an even better one. St. John Chrysostom, preaching more than sixteen hundred years ago, says as much: "As the apostles left their nets on being called, so she leaves her water jar to do the work of an evangelist by calling not one or two people, as Andrew and Philip did, but a whole city."[32] Bible scholar Father John Meier puts it bluntly: "Did

---

31. "The Samaritan woman's words of invitation ('Come, see,' 4:29) explicitly echo the witness of Philip in 1:46. . . . No less than Philip, she becomes a model for witness; in this case, however, she brings virtually an entire town. . . . The narrative thus places her on a par with Jesus' other disciples who brought his message to the world (cf. 17:20). . . . Granted, once they encounter Jesus for themselves, they are no longer dependent on her testimony (4:41–42) as they were at first (4:39); but it was likewise Nathanael's encounter with Jesus, not solely Philip's testimony, that led to Nathanael's confession (1:47–49). Like the Baptist and all other witnesses, she must now decrease so Christ, the object of faith, may increase (cf. 3:30)." Craig S. Keener, *The Gospel of John: A Commentary*, vol. 1 (Grand Rapids, MI: Baker Academic, 2003), 622–23.

32. John Chrysostom, "Homilies on the Gospel of John," 34.1, in *Ancient Christian Commentary on Scripture: New Testament*, vol. IVa, John 1–10, ed. Joel C. Elowsky, (Downers Grove, IL: InterVarsity Press, 2006),166.

the historical Jesus have women disciples? In name, no; in reality . . . yes. Certainly, the reality rather than the label would have been what caught most people's attention."[33]

Why then doesn't the Gospel come out and say "woman disciple" explicitly? The reason is that during the time of Jesus' ministry, there was no specific terminology in Aramaic to denote a female disciple.[34] It is only in St. Luke's new composition, the Acts of the Apostles, where we find the Greek word for female disciple (*mathētria*), not because the reality of female disciples didn't exist as Jesus walked upon the earth, but because Jesus Himself seems to have invented the reality. "Jesus indeed had committed women followers," Father Meier affirms, "but there was literally no feminine noun [in Aramaic] that could be used to describe them; there was no noun that said 'female disciple(s).' . . . New realities emerge on the historical scene before there are new words to describe them, and sometimes the time-lag between new reality and new coinage is lengthy."[35] Today then, the lag of language having long caught up with the reality that Jesus Himself presents in the Scriptures, we can confidently affirm that St. Photina is a disciple whom we, striving to live as disciples today, would do well to imitate.

Let us pray: *Dear Lord, You have given us the glorious example of St. Photina and her fellow Samaritans. When she encountered You, You overcame her shame and gave her the courage to proclaim Your salvation to all whom she knew. Sweet Jesus, please grant us the same fervor, faith, and fortitude that You granted to her. Amen.*

33. John P. Meier, *A Marginal Jew: Rethinking the Historical Jesus, Companions and Competitors* (New Haven, London: Yale University Press, 2001), 3:79.
34. Meier, *A Marginal Jew*, 3:79.
35. Meier, *A Marginal Jew*, 3:79.

GOING DEEPER

Seeing St. Photina come to believe in Jesus through her personal encounter with Him, we want to (1) *encounter* Him ourselves and (2) *witness* to Him as passionate disciples.

Answers or possible answers are found on pages 94–96. But ponder the questions for yourself, or share with your Bible study group before giving the answers a look.

- Where do you find yourself as a disciple today? Has anything changed since you started this book?

Remember the history of the hatred between the Jews and the Samaritans (pages 35–36).

- What does Jesus' inviting Samaritans into discipleship teach us about discipleship? Does this invitation make you think of any certain person whom Jesus might be calling you to reach out to in your own life?

Read John 4:39–42; then discuss these questions in your group, or ponder them on your own.

- What did the Samaritans do after they heard the woman's witness? What might have made them ready to do that?
- What was the result of Jesus' encounter with the Samaritans as He remained with them? Why do you think they might have responded in these ways?

Read John 4:16–30; then discuss these questions in your group, or ponder them on your own.

- St. Photina's own story, even the sinful parts, was an aspect of her witness: "Come, see a man who told me all that I ever did." (John 4:29a). How do you think it might have felt for her to share her faith when everyone in the town knew her sin? Using the virtues of prudence and of courage, how might Jesus be asking you to share parts of your story with others in witness to Him?

- St. Photina had to encounter Jesus personally to begin a relationship with Him. The other Samaritans began to believe because of her witness, but they also had to encounter Jesus and believe for themselves. Do you encounter Jesus regularly in your life? If not, where might be a good place to start?

- After walking through the true story of St. Photina and her fellow Samaritans, how do you feel? How can the other people in your Bible study (or your other friends) pray for you?

5

Work to *Remain* | John 6

You've begun the path of discipleship. You believe in Jesus. What's next? By now you can repeat in your sleep that believing leads to remaining. But what does it take to remain? John 6 begins to develop our answer.

Work and Gift | John 6:1–45

At the beginning of John 6, we see a large crowd following Jesus "because they saw the signs which he did on those who were diseased" (John 6:2). We've seen signs before. Sometimes they lead to the faith of a true disciple, and other times those who see the signs choose to stop at belief in the signs, not taking the next step to belief in Jesus. To these beginning believers, Jesus gave another sign: He feeds over five thousand people with just five loaves of bread and two fish (John 6:1–14)! The people realize that Jesus is the prophet like Moses and therefore is the Messiah.[36]

During the night after the multiplication of the loaves, Jesus and the disciples take a boat to the other side of the lake. The crowd follows them. They make their way to the other side of the lake—which

---

36. Deuteronomy 18:18, 15; Francis Martin and William Wright, *The Gospel of John* in *Catholic Commentary on Sacred Scripture* (Grand Rapids, MI: Baker Academic, 2015), 116.

is not an easy task—so that they can be with Jesus. But when they arrive, Jesus shows them that their sights are set too low. They had put in all that effort to get across the lake so that Jesus would give them more bread, whereas Jesus wants to give them eternal life. "Do not labor for the food which perishes," He tells them, "but for the food which remains [*ménō*] to eternal life, which the Son of man will give to you" (John 6:27).[37] They have begun to believe, but it requires something additional for that belief to mature into remaining. What we should take away from this vivid scene is that true discipleship requires effort on our part.

And yet, at the same time, it is impossible to earn relationship with God by our own human effort. In the end, faith and relationship with Jesus are God's gifts to us. The Father gives us the bread from heaven that, when we eat of it, empowers us to remain into eternal life: "Amen, amen, I say to you . . . my Father gives you the true bread from heaven. For the bread of God is that which comes down from heaven, and gives life to the world" (John 6:32–33; see also verse 27).[38] The crowds cry out for this bread. Like the woman of Samaria who desired the living water, they desire the bread of life. But will they also do the work involved in choosing to believe? Jesus gives them the opportunity, revealing plainly that He is this bread that will give them eternal life: "I am the bread of life; he who comes to me shall not hunger, and he who believes [*pisteúō*] in me shall never thirst" (John 6:35).[39] The problem is that even though the crowd has physically come to Him, they have not interiorly come to Him by doing the work of believing. Essentially, the crowd is in it for the freebies. Like those who come to church on Ash Wednesday for the

---

37. RSV-2CE translation adjusted by the author, based upon the Greek text (NA28).
38. RSV-2CE translation adjusted by the author, based upon the Greek text (NA28).
39. Notice that, at least in this passage, Jesus uses the phrase "comes to me" to mean the same thing as believing in Him.

blessed ashes but skip confession and leave before Communion, they are focused on the less important free meal and miss out on the greatest of God's gifts.

And, in it for the freebies, they murmur, grumble, complain, and gossip among themselves when Jesus does not give them what they want. Thinking that they know all that there is to know about Jesus, they refuse to learn from and believe in Him. "Every one who has heard and learned [*mathōn*] from the Father comes to me," Jesus says (John 6:45). A disciple, at the most basic level, is a learner. Believing the words of the teacher, the disciple learns from and lives like Him. This doesn't happen all at once. We grow from ignorance to experience by thousands of tiny steps. But Jesus is making it clear that learning, which is to say deepening our belief, is an essential part of the work of becoming and being a disciple. Only when we do the work of believing—imploring God for the gift of faith and diligently applying our minds to the study of His Word—are our souls enlarged to the proper capacity for receiving the freely given grace of remaining into eternal life.

Believing or Eating: Which Gives Eternal Life? | John 6:47–59

Speaking of eternal life, Jesus assures us that "whoever believes [*pisteúō*] has eternal life" (John 6:47b).[40] Yet just four verses later, Jesus also says that eating the bread that He gives is what merits eternal life (John 6:51–55). Which is it?

In truth, it is both: "Do not work for the food which perishes," Jesus says, "but for the food which remains [*ménō*] into eternal life. . . . This is the work of God, that you believe [*pisteúō*] in him whom he has sent" (John 6:27–29).[41] The work of belief leads to

---

40. English Standard Version, Catholic Edition.

the gift of remaining into eternal life. Remaining is not separate from believing. Instead, it is its natural completion, and to live forever, we must both believe in Jesus and eat that which empowers us to remain (John 6:27, 56).[42]

Finally, how does this food remain into eternal life? This food is eternal because it is Christ Himself. But Christ's being eternal doesn't do us any good unless we are somehow united to His eternity. Christ comes to us as "food that remains" so that the communion of eating His Flesh and drinking His Blood gives us a share in His own eternal life.[43] Yet this is not a onetime event. Bible scholar Craig Keener observes that when Jesus says, "he who eats my flesh"and "he who eats me" (John 6:54, 56, 57), the Greek form of *eats* really means something like "continues to subsist."[44] That means that the disciple who perseveres is able to constantly draw spiritual nourishment from his communion with Jesus. By regularly consuming the Body and Blood of Jesus, the disciple remains in Him, and He in the disciple, through any and every trial. It is to the disciple's first major "trial" or "test"—the same word in Greek—to which we now turn.

A Trial in Discipleship | John 6:60–71

Jesus' invitation to eat His Flesh and drink His Blood forced upon the disciples a difficult moment of decision that constituted a trial, or testing, of their discipleship:

Many of his disciples [*mathētēs*], when they heard it, said, "This is a hard saying; who can listen to it?" But Jesus, knowing in himself

---

41. RSV-2CE translation adjusted by the author, based upon the Greek text (NA28).

42. See Charles Kingsley Barrett, *The Gospel according to St. John: An Introduction and Commentary with Notes on the Greek Text*, 2nd ed. (Philadelphia: The Westminster Press, 1978), 286.

43. Barrett, *The Gospel according to St. John*, 286.

44. Craig S. Keener, *The Gospel of John: A Commentary*, 2 vols. (Grand Rapids, MI: Baker Academic, 2003), 691.

that his disciples [*mathētēs*] murmured at it, said to them, "Are you scandalized? . . . It is the spirit that gives life, the flesh is of no avail; the words that I have spoken to you are spirit and life. But there are some of you that do not believe [*pisteúō*]." For Jesus knew from the first who those were that did not believe [*pisteúō*], and who it was that would betray him.[45]

Many fail the test. Losing what faith they had, they do not remain with Jesus. They choose to walk away (John 6:66). The Twelve (or at least the Eleven), however, do genuinely believe. While St. John does not here use the term *remain*, it is obvious that the Twelve do at least physically remain with Him. They have not walked away, and they will receive His Flesh and Blood at the Last Supper. Jesus engages the Twelve who have remained, saying,

> "Will you also go away?" Simon Peter answered him, "Lord, to whom shall we go? You have the words of eternal life; and we have believed [*pisteúō*], and have come to know, that you are the Holy One of God." Jesus answered them, "Did I not choose you, the twelve, and one of you is a devil?" He spoke of Judas the son of Simon Iscariot, for he, one of the twelve, was to betray him. (John 6:67–71)

Spoiler alert: the Twelve remain. But the story is not over.

This scene drives home the point that discipleship is a process. The disciples don't understand; they still have room to grow, and it is also true that even now they can turn away. Eleven of them will fall in varying degrees before they return. Judas will betray Him, not return, and "go to his own place" (Acts 1:25). Perhaps he began to doubt even here as Jesus promised His Flesh and Blood, allowing his faith to slowly fade until "he immediately went out, and it was night." (John 13:30).

---

45. RSV-2CE translation adjusted by the author, based upon the Greek text (NA28).

The other Eleven make mistakes and nearly always misunderstand Jesus. Yet they hold to the faith, even when they don't understand. Perhaps it is even more impressive that they don't remain with Jesus because they understand; they remain because they have a personal relationship with Jesus. They are willing and working to learn from Him. This is what real discipleship looks like for them and for us. And, just as Jesus delighted in their progress, so too does Jesus delight in ours, even as He fixes our blunders, picks us up when we fall, and corrects our misunderstandings. With eyes fixed upon Jesus our hope, we who believe and remain are His disciples and will continue to live this reality more and more fully as we persevere along the path to eternal life.

Let us pray: *Loving Master, we believe in You who invite us to remain into eternal life by partaking of Your own Body and Blood. Give us devotion to Your Eucharistic presence; draw us close to You; and sustain us in every trial, that we might remain ever close to Your Sacred Heart. Amen.*

GOING DEEPER

The Main Thing: Listening to Jesus' teaching in John 6, we want to work to remain in Him by (1) learning from Him and (2) receiving the gift of His Flesh and Blood.

Answers or possible answers are found on pages 96–99. But ponder the questions for yourself, or share with your Bible study group before giving the answers a look.

- Where do you find yourself as a disciple today? Has anything changed since you started this book?

Read John 6:25–34; then discuss these questions in your group, or ponder them on your own.

- Why does the crowd cross the sea in search of Jesus? What is the work that Jesus wants them to do?

- The crowd following Jesus seems to be in it for the freebies. What are you in it for? Why do you come to relationship with Jesus? Remembering that each one of us on this side of heaven has mixed motivations, how, if at all, do you want your motivations to grow and change?

Read John 6:40–47; then discuss these questions in your group, or ponder them on your own.

- What is the will of the Father? Do you believe what Jesus says in John 6:40? What are some of the obstacles to believing this revelation for yourself and/or for others?

- What do the Jews in this scene do when Jesus reveals the will of the Father? How, in your life, do you act similarly? What is one thing that you can do this week that would help you have a little more trust in Jesus?

- A disciple learns from Jesus—from God. What are some good ways to learn from and about our Lord?

Read John 6:52–59 and the Catechism of the Catholic Church, *§1335–1336 and 1410–1419; then discuss these questions in your group, or ponder them on your own.*

- In John 6, what does Jesus say that we must do to remain in Him, and for Him to remain in us? According to Jesus, is consuming His Body and Blood necessary for life? What implications does this have for our lives?

Read John 6:69–71 and John 13:21–30; then discuss these questions in your group, or ponder them on your own.

- Where is your faith most vulnerable? Which is the hardest teaching, revealed by God, for you to believe? What is one thing you can do this week to learn more and strengthen your faith?

- After learning about the work of remaining and the importance of receiving the Body and Blood of Jesus for discipleship, how do you feel? How can the other people in your Bible study group (or your other friends) pray for you?

6

Perseverance Leads to *Devotion* | John 9

In the ninth chapter of his Gospel, St. John gives us the example of a man who began to be a disciple and then, persevering in the faith that he had received from Jesus, deepened his discipleship. The experience of this man shows clearly that becoming a true disciple is not a sudden, onetime event but is instead a growth in knowledge, trust of, and relationship with Jesus. So let us turn to the true story of a model disciple, the man born blind, and learn from him.[46]

Work and Witness | John 9:1–18

When Jesus and His disciples see the blind man for the first time, Jesus explains that the man was born blind so that "the works of God might be made manifest in him" (John 9:3; see also John 6:29). Jesus' intention is to inspire belief through the secondary work of healing the man of his blindness.

Jesus heals him using clay and then sends him to wash in the pool of Siloam (which means "sent"). The clay serves as a reminder of the

---

46. Rudolf Schnackenburg, *The Gospel according to St. John*, trans. Cecily Hastings, Francis McDonagh, David Smith, and Richard Foley, *Herder's Theological Commentary on the New Testament* (New York: Herder and Herder, 1980), Vol. 2:208.

creation of humanity, and the washing is symbolic of baptism.[47] In the act of receiving this "baptism," the novice disciple is *sent*, which foreshadows the witness-bearing task of the disciple. Disciples, then, are sent. We are to understand that this is our directive, too.

The man healed of his blindness causes quite a stir in his community. His neighbors ask, "Is not this the man who used to sit and beg?" He tells them that "the man called Jesus" healed him (John 9:8, 11). He doesn't yet know that Jesus is more than a man, but he is willing to tell his neighbors that Jesus, whoever He is, has done him a great favor.

The Pharisees don't know what to make of it either. Some are inspired by the miracle to think that Jesus is from God, whereas others think that He is disobeying God by doing the miracle on the Sabbath. When they ask the formerly blind man his opinion, he replies, "He is a prophet" (John 9:17). Apparently he reflected more deeply upon the sign and recognized the miracle-working Jesus as a prophet. As St. Augustine puts it, "Not yet anointed in heart, he could not confess the Son of God. Nevertheless, he is not wrong in what he says either."[48]

Many of the people, however, "did not believe [*pisteúo*] that he had been blind and had received his sight, until they called the parents of the man who had received his sight" (John 9:18). They stubbornly resist the signs before their eyes. Bible scholar Father Rudolf

---

47. Scott Hahn, "Temple, Sign, and Sacrament: Towards a New Perspective on the Gospel of John," *Letter and Spirit* 4 (2008): 126–27; Augustine, *Commentary on the Gospel of John*, 44:1–2; Michael J. Wilkins, *Following the Master: A Biblical Theology of Discipleship* (Grand Rapids: MI, Zondervan, 1992), 221.

48. Schnackenburg, *John*, 2:248; cf. Raymond E. Brown, *Gospel according to John I—XII* (New Haven, CT: Yale University Press, 1966), 373; Charles Kingsley Barrett, *The Gospel according to St. John: An Introduction with Commentary and Notes on the Greek Text*, 2nd ed. (Philadelphia: The Westminster Press, 1978), 360; Augustine, "Tractates on the Gospel of John," 44.9, in *Ancient Christian Commentary on Scripture: New Testament, John 1—10*, ed. Joel C. Elowsky, (Downers Grove, IL: InterVarsity Press, 2006), 1A:373.

Bultmann suggests that St. John "seeks to portray the struggle of darkness against light, and to show the sacrifice which is implied in the decision of faith."[49] In other words, the man—and each disciple—will have to remain in his belief through whatever trials beset him. Will the formerly blind man allow his belief to continue to deepen, or will he too shrink in fear at the threat of being cast out?

Persevering Belief | John 9:18–25

After summoning the man's parents, whose fear prevented them from seeking faith in Jesus, the Pharisees again interrogate the formerly blind man. They give the appearance of diligently seeking the truth about Jesus but have already made up their minds that they consider Him to be a sinner. These Pharisees chose darkness rather than light when they rejected the freeing truth of Jesus. They rendered themselves unable to believe because they refused to accept the ways that the Scriptures witness to Jesus.[50] Rather than be open to faith and discipleship themselves, the Pharisees switch tactics by focusing on trying to shake the faith of the formerly blind man. They say, "Give God the praise" (John 9:24) which, in the Old Testament, is a phrase used to encourage sinners to confess their sins and repent.[51] The Pharisees are doing the opposite of what they say. This new disciple is already giving God praise by bearing witness to Jesus and, as we will soon see, is willing to glorify God even more by suffering for Him.[52]

If the formerly blind man had bent to the pressure of the Pharisees, he would have failed to praise God in truth because he would have put the glory of men before the glory of God.[53] He is more

---

49. Rudolf Bultmann, *The Gospel of John: A Commentary*, trans G. R. Beasley-Murray (Oxford: Basil Blackwell, 1971), 334–35.

50. John 9:24b, 4–5; 8:31–32; 5:38; Bultmann, *Gospel of John*, 335.

51. Joshua 7:19; 1 Samuel 6:5; 2 Chronicles 30:8; Jeremiah 13:16; Schnackenburg, *Gospel according to St. John*, 2:251.

52. John 12:23–24; 21:19.

courageous than his parents and is an example of courage for future disciples like us. The Jews of John 5:44 (perhaps some of the same men as those persecuting the formerly blind man now) receive glory from one another but do not seek the glory/praise that comes from God (*glory* and *praise* in these passages are the same word in Greek, *doxa*). The formerly blind man, on the other hand, does not seek glory or praise from men but instead gives glory and praise to God by his honesty and his openness to believe. He doesn't yet know anything about Jesus' moral character; he just knows what Jesus accomplished for him: "Whether he is a sinner, I do not know; one thing I know, that though I was blind, now I see" (John 9:25).

This confession, too, is a step toward discipleship. With faith greater than the Pharisees' and many of his neighbors', he believes the works that Jesus does in His Father's name—works that bear *witness* to Jesus. The formerly blind man may not yet believe *in Jesus*, but his belief *in the works* reminds us of these later words of Jesus: "If I am not doing the works of my Father, then do not believe me; but if I do them, even though you do not believe [*pisteúō*] me, believe [*pisteúō*] the works, that you may know and understand that the Father is in me and I am in the Father" (John 10:37–38).[54] Many times, that initial witness that sparks our faith is another person. But sometimes the witness is a miracle or an insight coming out of nowhere, or events that couldn't have been mere coincidence. The formerly blind man believed in the work that Jesus had done for him and, despite pressure from the powerful Pharisees, held on to that faith with tenacity.

He still doesn't believe that Jesus is God. He probably has a lot of questions. But he believes as much as he can with the experience and information he has. He has seen the works of Jesus and knows

---

53. John 12:42–43.
54. See also John 5:36; 10:25.

that something special is here, even though he can't yet put his finger on just what that something is. Maybe you struggle to believe in Jesus—or in God at all—but something stirs in you when you see His disciples serving the poor, or enter a beautiful cathedral, or read the writings of the saints and theologians, or experience *something* sometimes when you try to pray. Believe in that first. Then, when you can, offer a little prayer: "Jesus, if You really are there and really are God, I want to believe in You. Show me, if You are." If this is where you are, you're acting like this model disciple and are already a novice disciple because you are invested in learning from Jesus' works.

Disciple of Jesus | John 9:26–41

Still under questioning by the Pharisees—questioning that forces him to reflect upon his experience again and again—the formerly blind man becomes so convinced that Jesus comes from God that he declares himself to be a disciple. Not only that, but he even asks the Pharisees if they, too, want to become disciples of Jesus, which St. Cyril of Alexandria teaches us "reveals his own state of mind that he was not only willing to become, but actually had already become, a disciple."[55] As a disciple, he now takes control of the conversation. Convinced that Jesus comes from God, he sends the Pharisees onto their heels in anger. "You," they say with contempt, "are a disciple [*mathētēs*] of that one, but we are disciples [*mathētēs*] of Moses" (John 9:28).[56] A clear contrast has arisen between a disciple of Jesus and a group of "antidisciples" who call themselves disciples of Moses.

55. Cyril of Alexandria, *Commentary on the Gospel of John*, 6.1, in *Ancient Christian Commentary on Scripture: New Testament*, vol. IVA, *John 1—10*, ed. Joel C. Elowsky (Downers Grove, IL: InterVarsity Press, 2006), 332, emphasis added.
56. RSV-2CE translation adjusted by the author based upon the Greek text (NA28); Charles Kingsley Barrett, *The Gospel according to St. John: An Introduction and Commentary with Notes on the Greek Text*, 2nd ed. (Philadelphia: The Westminster Press, 1978), 362; Schnackenburg, *The Gospel according to St. John*, 2:251.

But there should be no conflict between being a disciple of Moses and a disciple of Jesus. As Jesus Himself said to another group of unbelievers: "If you believed [*pisteúō*] Moses, you would believe [*pisteúō*] me, for he wrote of me" (John 5:46). "Their appeal to Moses," Bible scholar Rudolf Bultmann writes, "was turned into an accusation against them, so it is with the words of the healed man. . . . For precisely their knowledge of God, which they claim to enjoy as disciples of Moses, should lead them to accept this proof of Jesus' authority."[57] Presumably this Jewish blind man also considered himself a disciple of Moses. What, then, is the difference between him, a disciple of Jesus, and these Pharisees who show themselves to be "antidisciples"?

The answer is, by this point, unsurprising. The formerly blind man *believes*—first in the miracle and then in Jesus Himself—whereas the Pharisees, though unable to deny the miracle, do not allow themselves to believe that the miracle is wrought by the power of God and thus they never come to believe in Jesus. The formerly blind man perseveres in this belief through suffering, such that he can be said to remain; whereas for the Pharisees, it is their guilt that remains. (See John 9:41.) Since they fail to believe in Jesus, Jesus does not remain with them. Instead, their guilt remains because they act against Jesus by trying to talk and threaten this new disciple into denying his faith.

However, the Pharisees' efforts to shake the man's faith fail. In fact, their persecution has only served to strengthen his conviction. Therefore, force takes over and the formerly blind man's confession causes him to be cast out (from the presence of the Pharisees and probably even from the Jewish community that gathered in the synagogues). His encounter with Jesus, who healed his sight, has apparently given him the courage that his parents did not have (John 9:18–23).

---

57. Bultmann, *The Gospel of John: A Commentary*, 366–67.

Soon, Jesus comes to find His new disciple. Because he did not fall under the weight of his fear, he was able to encounter Jesus again and take the next step in his belief. Perseverance through a trial leads to deeper belief. We all go through trials—for some of us they are primarily internal, and for others of us more typically they are external. Whatever the trial and however long, Jesus always comes to find us at the end. He comes with His consolation, even if it takes years or a whole lifetime, and shows us how experiencing darkness has allowed us to grow in love and relationship with Him. For his part, the formerly blind man has gone as far as Old Testament faith and honest reflection on what Jesus has done can take him. Now, like Nathanael and Photina before him, he must encounter Jesus personally so that he can have faith in the One who fulfills his longing for the Messiah.[58]

Finding the man, Jesus asks, "Do you believe [*pisteúō*] in the Son of Man?" He answers, "And who is he, sir [*kyrios*], that I may believe [*pisteúō*] in him?" to which Jesus responds, "You have seen him, and it is he who speaks to you." The formerly blind new disciple bows down before Jesus in faith, proclaiming, "'Lord [*kyrios*], I believe [*pisteúō*]'; and he worshiped him" (John 9:35–38). Discipleship does not come in the coldness of unattached intellectual speculation but in the warmth of a loving relationship. Yes, using our minds is critical. We see the formerly blind man grow in his discipleship by reflecting rationally on his experience. But remaining, as it is expressed here by persevering in one's belief even through suffering, leads to loving devotion, which this man shows as he bows down before Jesus.

He "bows down before" Jesus. Or, as some translations give it, the formerly blind man "worships" Him. Both are valid translations of the original Greek word *proskynéō*, which definitely means that the man

---

58. Schnackenburg, *The Gospel according to St. John*, 2:253.

lay prostrate on the ground before Jesus, perhaps even kissing His feet or the hem of His garment. He is neither an impartial observer nor a stoic scholar of Jesus' words and actions. The formerly blind man shows us that persevering/remaining in the faith moves us to worship the Lord with devotion. In fact, devotion is a clear mark of a disciple. One who does not follow the example of the blind man in worship has not yet become a full disciple of Jesus. She might be beginning the journey, but she cannot be said to have believed and remained.

What are some ways that we can follow the example of the man born blind? If we disciples want to remain/persevere into true discipleship, coming to devout worship of Jesus, we must work with Him to rightly order our souls:

- Before anything else, the man received grace from the Lord for his healing. We, too, must first pray to God for the graces we need. We ask Him for healing of past wounds and hurts, those we caused by our own sin and those inflicted upon us by others. We beg Him for freedom from the current sins that hold us bound by going to Reconciliation frequently. And we pray for the seven most important virtues: faith, hope, love, prudence, courage, temperance, and justice.

- After receiving grace from Jesus, the formerly blind man reflected upon what Jesus had done for him. We, too, must apply our intellects to our discipleship by reading good books and watching or listening to good media to foster prudence in our minds.

- But the man did not stay in his head; he took the courageous initiative to speak to others about his experience, even though he did not yet have it all figured out. We, too, should exercise courage in our hearts by witnessing to Jesus in all the ways that we can, not waiting until we think we are perfect or have it all figured out.

- Finally, this model disciple sets himself before Jesus in loving devotion. For our part, we can begin to root out those things that take our focus away from Jesus. We do so by engaging in fasts and sacrificing those things that tend to take our emotions down the wrong path. Small, consistent fasts and sacrifices foster the virtue of temperance in us so that the energy of our emotions may drive us toward the eternal life that comes when we remain in Jesus and His word.

Let us pray: *Divine Lord Jesus Christ, You have worked and continue to work wonders for Your people. Healing this man's bodily ailment, You worked the even greater miracle of placing persevering faith in his soul. His perseverance led him to worship, bowing down before You. Grant us this grace as well, generous Savior! May we remain in You by holding fast to the faith and may this abiding perseverance flower into devotion. Amen.*

GOING DEEPER

The Main Thing: Through the teaching of Jesus and the example of the man born blind, we see that (1) remaining in Jesus often looks like continuing to believe in the midst of suffering, and (2) this perseverance naturally leads to devotion. I will worship the God whom I have come to know in the storm.

Answers or possible answers are found on pages 99–101. But ponder the questions for yourself, or share with your Bible study group before giving the answers a look.

- Where do you find yourself as a disciple today? Has anything changed since you started this book?

Read John 9:6–12; then discuss these questions in your group, or ponder them on your own.

- What does Jesus do to heal the man of his blindness? What is the significance of these two actions?
- What does the word *Siloam* mean? Why is this significant? Does this have any implications for your life?

Read John 9:24–34; then discuss these questions in your group, or ponder them on your own.

- What do the Pharisees eventually do to the man? Why do they do this?
- The Pharisees challenged the man's faith. What are common challenges to a person's faith today? Which ones affect you? Is it hard or easy to call yourself a disciple of Jesus in public? What makes it so?
- Even before he believed in Jesus, the formerly blind man believed in the works that Jesus did, and this belief carried him in his trial. What are a few works that Jesus has done in your life—small or significant?

Read John 9:35–41; then discuss these questions in your group, or ponder them on your own.

- What does Jesus do when He hears that the Pharisees have cast out the formerly blind man? Has there ever been a time when you've felt particularly close to Jesus after a time of difficult struggles?

- What does the formerly blind man do when Jesus tells him that He is the Messiah? How could you respond to Jesus more like this model disciple? What are your biggest obstacles?

- After walking through the true story of the man born blind, how do you feel? How can the other people in your Bible study (or your other friends) pray for you?

7

Love One Another |
John 13—17

In John 1:19—12:50, Jesus acted publicly, often addressing His words and displaying His deeds to a broad audience as an invitation to believe in Him. In John 13—20, Jesus shifts focus. In these chapters He is almost exclusively speaking to those who already believe and have already begun to remain. He is encouraging them to continue to remain in Him through the even greater trials that are soon to come, and is explicitly revealing that to remain in Him is to share His communion with the Father and the Spirit.[59]

John 13—17 takes place at the Last Supper that was shared by Jesus and the Twelve. These are the men who stayed with Jesus even after many of His disciples drew back and no longer walked with Him. Now Jesus speaks to them about remaining in the context of the meal wherein, according to the other Gospels, He gives them His Body and Blood for the first time and focuses upon the relationship with God in which true disciples remain.[60]

---

59. Raymond E. Brown, *The Gospel according to John, XIII—XXI*, Anchor Yale Bible series, (New Haven, CT:, 1966), 542.

60. Rudolf Bultmann, *The Gospel of John: A Commentary*, trans. G. R. Beasley-Murray (Oxford: Basil Blackwell, 1971), 363, 457. Some may object to applying Jesus' teaching at the Last Supper to all disciples, noting that only the Twelve were present for the Last Supper (cf. Mark 14:17; Luke 22:14) and therefore contending that the

Home Forever | John 14:1–6, 15–17

Around the table, Jesus begins His longest recorded conversation with His disciples. He encourages them to believe (or trust) in Him and assures them that He is preparing a place for them to remain with Him forever.[61] "In my Father's house," Jesus says in our English Bibles, "are many rooms." However, His words reveal a deeper meaning when we consider that the Greek word for "room" (*monē*) means "remaining place."[62] At the beginning of the end of John's Gospel, as Jesus has His last conversation before His passion, we are brought back to the beginning of Jesus' ministry. "Rabbi," they had said to Him, "where do you remain [*ménō*]?" Jesus had replied, "Come and see" (John 1:38–39).[63] They did come, and they did see. For something like three years, they have been learning where Jesus really lives: *in His soul.* He remains in the communion of the Father and the Spirit always and forever. Soon He will remain there in His body as well. The amazing thing is that His disciples will be able to follow Him into the eternal joy of heaven. This is incredible! This is the entire goal of discipleship: to have an eternal "remaining place" in the house of the Father—Heaven—which is the communion of Father, Son, and Spirit. "The slave," Jesus had said, "does not remain [*ménō*] in the house forever; the son remains [*ménō*] *forever*" (John 8:35).[64]

---

teaching of the Last Supper Discourse applies only to them. It is also true that the only disciples mentioned by name in John's discourse are members of the Twelve. However, Jesus is here giving teaching applicable to all His disciples and the evangelist himself indicates this: John's usual designation of "Twelve" (*dōdeka*) is entirely absent from the Last Supper Discourse and, according to Bultmann, seems to be consciously avoided (Bultmann, *The Gospel according to John*, 458–59). In addition, Bultmann rightly points out that both John 13:35 and John 15:8 indicate that the teaching of this discourse is for all disciples (Bultmann, *The Gospel according to John*, 459, n. 1).

61. Remember that the Greek word *pisteúō* can be translated into English as "believe" or "trust."

62. The word *monē* is simply the noun form of the verb *menō*, "to remain," which we have seen throughout this book.

63. RSV-2CE translation adjusted by the author based upon the Greek text (NA28).

64. RSV-2CE translation adjusted by the author based upon the Greek text (NA28).

Believing in Jesus, we have been empowered to become children of God. No longer slaves of sin, we live in the freedom of sons and daughters who reside in their Father's house not just for a little while but *forever.*

To Believe and to Love | 1 John 3:23–24

Moreover, this promise of heavenly joy is not just for the future. We begin to live the goal of our discipleship even now, while we are still imperfect and still on the journey. If we love Jesus and express that love by keeping His commandments, the Holy Spirit remains—present tense—with us and in us, and will be with us *forever* (John 14:16–17). God's commandment, St. John tells us in his first letter, is "that we should believe [*pisteúō*] in the name of his Son Jesus Christ and love one another, just as he has commanded us" (1 John 3:23). If we believe and love, keeping His commandments, we will remain in the Holy Spirit. "All who keep his commandments," St. John writes, "remain [*ménō*] in him and he in them. And by this we know that he remains [*ménō*] in us, by the Spirit which he has given us" (1 John 3:24).[65] It's pretty easy to know whether or not we believe. But remaining is more abstract. So what is the evidence that we are remaining and are therefore true disciples?

The degree to which we believe and love is the degree to which we remain, and therefore the degree to which we are true disciples. As Jesus said, "By this all men will know that you are my disciples [*mathētēs*], if you have love for one another" (John 13:35).[66] The possible expressions of love are many, and each of us as a disciple is called to express that love in the ways and at the times that are available to us in our own lives. Maybe He is calling you to bring a particular person to

---

65. RSV-2CE translation adjusted by the author based upon the Greek text (NA28).
66. RSV-2CE translation adjusted by the author based upon the Greek text (NA28).

Him. Maybe He's calling someone else to spend more time in prayer. Maybe He's calling another to serve the poor or teach the young or speak boldly in the world. Whatever the particular mode, each of us as a disciple strengthens the joy of the Holy Spirit remaining within us as we choose to believe and to love.

Finally, all of this is not some magic formula for receiving gifts from the Holy Spirit. Rather, it is the pattern of relationship with God.[67] Remaining in relationship with Jesus naturally moves us to share in His mission to enfold each person in the world into the loving embrace of the Trinity. The true disciple of Jesus keeps the commandments with a heart desiring the joy that comes from being of one mind and one heart with God Himself, united even more closely than a vine to its branches.

Bearing Fruit | John 15:1–17

Using this image of the unity of a vine and its branches, Jesus takes us deeper into the meaning of remaining in Him:

> Remain [ménō] in me, and I in you. As the branch cannot bear fruit by itself, unless it remains [ménō] in the vine, neither can you, unless you remain [ménō] in me. I am the vine, you are the branches. He who remains [ménō] in me, and I in him, he it is that bears much fruit, for apart from me you can do nothing. If a man does not remain [ménō] in me, he is cast forth as a branch and withers; and the branches are gathered, thrown into the fire and burned. If you remain [ménō] in me, and my words remain [ménō] in you, ask whatever you will, and it shall be done for you. By this my Father is glorified, that you bear much fruit, and so prove to be my disciples [mathētēs]. (John 15:4–8)[68]

---

67. Craig S. Keener, *The Gospel of John: A Commentary*, 2 vols. (Grand Rapids, MI: Baker Academic, 2003), 972.
68. RSV-2CE translation adjusted by the author based upon the Greek text (NA28).

The branch gets all its life and power from the vine. It can bear fruit only if it remains attached; if it is detached from the vine, immediately it begins to die. Jesus the vine holds nothing back from us, the branches, and we are privileged to share His life totally and completely dependent upon Him. To remain in Jesus is to constantly draw life from intimate communion with Him, and this intimate communion is the core of Christianity.[69] True discipleship is the essence of Christian life.

This true discipleship always bears fruit in practical love. This fruitful discipleship, however, will come only with suffering.[70] "Every branch that does bear fruit [the Father] prunes," Jesus tells us, "that it may bear more fruit" (John 15:2). Fruit bearing is not a further step in discipleship, nor is it an optional activity. Rather, it is the organic evidence of remaining in Jesus and consequently the organic evidence of discipleship. Jesus does not say, "One must remain in me if he desires to bear fruit." Rather, Jesus says, "He who remains [*ménō*] in me, and I in him, he it is that bears much fruit, for apart from me you can do nothing" (John 15:5). The power to bear fruit comes from a living relationship with Jesus, the true vine.[71] Bible scholar Father Raymond Brown explains: "The sense is not that when the hearers bear fruit, they will become his disciples, but that in bearing fruit they show they are disciples. *Becoming or being a disciple is the same as being or remaining in Jesus.*"[72] In other words, someone who seems to be a disciple but who bears no fruit must have a significant deficiency in

69. Charles Kingsley Barrett, *The Gospel according to St. John: An Introduction and Commentary with Notes on the Greek Text*, 2nd ed. (Philadelphia: The Westminster Press, 1978), 470.
70. Rudolf Schnackenburg, *The Gospel according to St. John*, trans. Cecily Hastings, Francis McDonagh, David Smith, and Richard Foley, *Herder's Theological Commentary on the New Testament* (New York: Herder and Herder, 1968), 2:98.
71. The relationship must be mutual because a real relationship always involves multiple persons.
72. Brown, *John XIII—XXI*, 662–63; emphasis added.

his remaining with and in Jesus. This is part of a good examination of conscience for us: *Am I bearing fruit?*

Before we ask that question, though, we need to know what the fruit of discipleship looks like. Earlier I called this fruit "practical love" to emphasize that the fruit Jesus empowers us to bear is a love that *does something*; it's not just a feeling. This love is practical because it does two things: (1) It gives witness to Jesus for those who do not know Him, and (2) it builds up the Church. To say it another way, practical love both draws nonbelievers to Christ and invites current believers more deeply into His love. These goals are accomplished by the witness of word, example, service, and any other practical way in which one can show real love. In practical love, whether for those outside or inside the church, the disciple moves out of herself in generosity as a member of the Christian community, as a branch on the vine of the New Israel.[73] Real discipleship has no place for individualism. Instead, it brings one into communion with the Father, Son, and Spirit, moving one out into the mutual love that exists among Christians and the apostolic witness that brings others into the Christian family. Discipleship is essentially relational and essentially missionary; it is essentially ecclesial.[74] In this way, we see that bearing fruit is building up those brothers and sisters of ours who are already part of the church. Bearing fruit is also inviting those outside into this communion of the Father, Son, and Holy Spirit with all the people He has adopted in baptism.

---

73. The vine is a frequent symbol for Israel (the people of God) in the Old Testament. See, for instance, Brown, *John XIII—XXI*, 669–72, 674–76, 679–81. For the clearest Old Testament examples of Israel as vine, see Hosea 10:1, 14:7; Jeremiah 6:9; Ezekiel 15:1–6; 17:5–10; 19:10–14; Psalm 80:8–19.

74. John 14:1–3, 16–17, 23.

Let us pray: *Lord God, You teach us to love. You draw us into love by taking us up into the eternal communion of love that You are—Father, Son, and Holy Spirit. Your love is so deep that You prune from our souls those attitudes, habits, and desires that are contrary to love. Draw us deeper into Your love, we beg You, Lord God. Expand our hearts, and teach us to love our neighbors so that together we might live in Your joy now and forever. Amen.*

GOING DEEPER

Answers or possible answers are found on pages 101–102. But ponder the questions for yourself, or share with your Bible study group before giving the answers a look.

- Where do you find yourself as a disciple today? Has anything changed since you started this book?

Read John 14:1–4; then discuss these questions in your group, or ponder them on your own.

- At the beginning of John 14, what does Jesus ask His disciples to do? What are some common obstacles to doing that? What are the most common obstacles for you?

- What thoughts and emotions stir in your mind and heart as you think of Jesus preparing a place for you in heaven?

Read 1 John 3:23–24; then discuss these questions in your group, or ponder them on your own.

- What ways are you, as a disciple, naturally inclined to utilize in expressing love for others (examples: intercessory prayer, service to the poor, teaching others, pro-life work, etc.)? Are there any ways where God might be calling you to grow (maybe in different expressions or maybe with a greater dedication or intensity in the ways in which you are naturally inclined)?

Read John 15:1–17; then discuss these questions in your group, or ponder them on your own.

- What does the Father do for the branch that bears fruit? Why does He do this? What might this look like in the life of a disciple?

- What can a disciple do apart from Jesus? What happens with a disciple who remains in Jesus? Have you seen a difference in your life between being apart from Jesus and remaining in Him? What was the difference?

- According to this chapter, what are the two big-picture ways in which disciples bear fruit? What are one or two practical ways in which you can focus on each of these ways of fruit bearing?

- After learning about the "remaining place" that Jesus prepares for you, being invited to remain united to Him as His friend, and hearing Jesus' image of the vine and the branches, how do you feel? How can the other people in your Bible study (or your other friends) pray for you?

8

The Beloved Disciple | John 19—21

Our journey through the Gospel of John has shown us multiple models of discipleship. We have also learned what it means to be a disciple from the words and actions of Jesus. Now, at the end of the Gospel, we can put together everything that we've learned by looking at the man known as the Beloved Disciple, whom scholars consider to be the Gospel's portrait of an ideal disciple.[75]

Standing at the Foot of the Cross | John 19:25–37

The Beloved Disciple was present at the Last Supper, and because of this, we know that he believes in Jesus and has at least started to remain in Him. However, even the Twelve had a long way to go in

---

75. See, for instance, Charles Kingsley Barrett, *The Gospel according to St. John: An Introduction and Commentary with Notes on the Greek Text*, 2nd ed. (Philadelphia: The Westminster Press, 1978), 588; Rudolf Schnackenburg, *The Gospel according to St. John*, trans. Cecily Hastings, Francis McDonagh, David Smith, and Richard Foley, *Herder's Theological Commentary on the New Testament* (New York: Herder and Herder, 1968), 2:378; Craig S. Keener, *The Gospel of John: A Commentary*, 2 vols. (Grand Rapids, MI: Baker Academic, 2003), 656, 1144; and Melvyn R. Hillmer, "They Believed in Him: Discipleship in the Johannine Tradition," in *Patterns of Discipleship in the New Testament*, ed. Richard N. Longenecker (Grand Rapids, MI: Eerdmans, 1996), 89.

their discipleship. When Jesus was arrested, they all fled. Peter followed for a while, but eventually he denied Jesus and went away. The Beloved Disciple, though, came back to be with Jesus in His final agony. The Beloved Disciple and the women were the only ones strong enough to be with Jesus at the Cross. Even though the word "remain" (*ménō*) is not used in John 19, the Beloved Disciple's action of being with Jesus at the foot of the cross clearly shows his persevering belief in Jesus, even throughout the greatest of trials. Bible scholar Father Rudolf Schnackenburg connects the disciple's perseverance at the foot of the cross with his believing in John 20 and his remaining in John 21:

> The severest test of faith [is] the Passion of Jesus. . . . Only "the disciple whom Jesus loved" holds out steadfastly under the Cross (19:26f.), "and he too is the first to understand the signs of the Resurrection," when he "saw and believed" (20:8). Thus, he appears as the ideal embodiment of the believer who knows his Lord, who perseveres by his side, who recognizes him in his hidden manifestation (as again in the epilogue, 21:7) and hence also is given the promise that he will "remain" till the Lord comes (cf. 21:22f.)—all of which, no doubt, constitutes on a deeper level a lesson for the believing community.[76]

Commenting upon this perseverance through this most severe trial, St. Jerome praises the Beloved Disciple as "the only one of the apostles bold enough to take his stand before the cross."[77] For his boldness, he is rewarded with sight of the fulfillment of the Scriptures in the mystery of the blood and water flowing forth from the side of Jesus. Thus,

---

76. Rudolf Schnackenburg, *The Gospel according to St. John*, trans. Kevyn Smyth, *Herder's Theological Commentary on the New Testament* (New York: Herder and Herder, 1968), 1:572.

77. Jerome, Letter 127.5, in *Ancient Christian Commentary on Scripture: New Testament*, vol. IVA, *John 11—21*, ed. Joel C. Elowsky (Downers Grove, IL: InterVersity Press, 2006), 320.

as we learn in John 19:35, he is able to bear witness that others, too, might believe. His action of remaining at the foot of the cross bears fruit in the practical love of witness to others.[78] We, too, must pray for the grace to be steadfast like the Beloved Disciple at the foot of the cross, letting nothing turn us from our devotion to Jesus.

"He Took Her into his Own" | John 19:27

The Beloved Disciple isn't the only person at the foot of the cross. Next to him is Mary, the mother of Jesus. Jesus entrusts the Beloved Disciple to Mary, and Mary to the Beloved Disciple, who takes her "into his own" (John 19:27).[79] What does it mean to take Mary into his own? As Pope St. John Paul II teaches, "Clearly, in the Greek text the expression *eis ta idia* ['into his own'; John 19:27] goes beyond the mere acceptance of Mary by the disciple in the sense of material lodging and hospitality in his house; it indicates rather a communion of life established between the two as a result of the words of the dying Christ."[80] Mary and the Beloved Disciple live out the fruits of their steadfast remaining with Jesus in the practical love of supporting one another.

Furthermore, since the Beloved Disciple is the model, those of us who love as disciples today would be wise to take Christ's own mother into the communion of our own lives. Like the Beloved Disciple, we meet her particularly at the foot of the cross where she comes to point us to her Son and comfort us in our own suffering. Mary teaches the disciple what to do with his sorrow as his own heart is pierced in

---

78. Barret notes that while the text is not explicit that it is the Beloved Disciple who bears witness, the context makes such a reasonable assumption (*Gospel according to St. John*, 557).
79. RSV-2CE translation adjusted by the author based upon the Greek text (NA28).
80. John Paul II, Encyclical Letter, *Redemptoris Mater* (March 25, 1987), http://w2.vatican.va/content/john-paul-ii/en/encyclicals/documents/ hf_jp-ii_enc_25031987_redemptoris-mater.html, note 130, emphasis added.

agony. Who better than she to do this? After all, she was the first to tread the path of Christian suffering with Jesus, as is made clear in the prophesy of Simeon in the Gospel of Luke: "Simeon blessed them and said to Mary his mother, 'Behold, this child is set for the fall and rising of many in Israel, and for a sign that is spoken against (and a sword will pierce through your own soul also), that thoughts out of many hearts may be revealed'" (Luke 2:34–35). Since Mary is alive with Jesus in heaven, it is wise for us to pray that she intercede for us to be able to stand with Jesus in steadfast devotion through the trials of life as she and the Beloved Disciple stood with Him in His suffering on the cross.

At the Tomb: The Disciple Who Believes | John 20:1–10

Three days after the Beloved Disciple stands at the foot of the cross, he and Peter receive word that the tomb of Jesus is empty. They run to the tomb. He follows Peter inside, sees, and believes. But what does he believe as he sees the inside of the tomb on that first Easter morning? The Gospel tells us, "Then the other disciple, who reached the tomb first, also went in, and he saw and believed [*pisteúō*]; for as yet they did not know the Scripture, that he must rise from the dead" (John 20:8–9). In this case, the Greek form of the verb "believe" (*pisteúō*) is probably better translated "began to believe."[81] Although our model disciple did believe, and he had remained with Jesus at His cross, even he had room to grow in his discipleship. Even he would not attain

---

81. Francis Martin and William M. Wright IV, *The Gospel of John* (*Catholic Commentary on Sacred Scripture*) (Grand Rapids, MI: Baker Academic, 2015). In this sentence, the Greek verb form of the verb *believe* (*pisteúō*) (aorist active indicative) can be translated, they write, as "began to believe." When expressing the full Easter faith of those who have seen the risen Jesus, however (John 20:18, 25, 29), the evangelist tends to use the perfect tense. The Beloved Disciple at the tomb does, then, possess true Easter faith, but Easter faith that is yet incomplete.

full Easter faith until he actually saw for himself the risen Jesus. No matter how far we have come, there will always be room to grow. As disciples, we are always humbly in process.

On the Seashore: The Disciple Who Remains | John 21:20–25

The Beloved Disciple had passed from the beginnings of belief at the tomb to full Easter faith when he sees Jesus resurrected in person, and soon after, Jesus made it clear that He wanted him to remain.

A small group of disciples goes fishing with Peter. At the end of a long night of work and having caught very few fish, Jesus calls out from the seashore to the frustrated fishermen. The Beloved Disciple is the first to recognize the voice of his teacher. "It is the Lord!" he exclaims to his brothers (John 21:7). They come ashore and have breakfast. Jesus and Peter have a conversation that includes mention of the Beloved Disciple's remaining:

> Peter turned and saw following them the disciple [*mathētēs*] whom Jesus loved, who had lain close to his breast at the supper . . . [and] said to Jesus, "Lord, what about this man?" Jesus said to him, "If it is my will that he remain [*ménō*] until I come, what is that to you? . . . This is the disciple [*mathētēs*] who is bearing witness to these things, and who has written these things; and we know that his witness is true." (John 21:20–24)[82]

What Jesus probably means here is that this disciple bears "fruit which remains [*ménō*]" (John 15:16) and that fruit is the Gospel of John itself. The witness of the Gospel is the proof and natural consequence of this one man's discipleship. Standing at the foot of the cross with steadfast devotion, he bears witness to the suffering and death by which the Lord saved us, and writes all that he has written about Jesus

---

82. RSV-2CE translation adjusted by the author based upon the Greek text (NA28).

so that we who read the Gospel might believe (John 19:35). For two thousand years, this fruit of discipleship has remained! What will be the fruit of your discipleship?

Let us pray: *Lord Jesus, risen from the dead, You have taken us on this journey of discipleship and given us models to guide our way. Like the Beloved Disciple, may we remain steadfastly beside You in suffering, believe with joyful alacrity, and bear lasting fruit in our witness to others. Be with us now and always. Amen.*

GOING DEEPER

Answers or possible answers are found on pages 102–104. But ponder the questions for yourself, or share with your Bible study before giving the answers a look.

- Where do you find yourself as a disciple today? Has anything changed since you started this book?

Read John 19:25–37. Let yourself feel the emotion of the scene. Imagine yourself there with Jesus and Mary and the Beloved Disciple if you can. Then discuss these questions in your group, or ponder them on your own.

- What thoughts and emotions come up as you look upon Jesus crucified in your imagination? How might Jesus be calling you to bear witness to this love of His in the world?
- What is your relationship with Mary like? Are there any struggles in that relationship? How could you open your heart a little more to heed the Gospel's invitation to take her into your own?

Read John 20:1–10; then discuss these questions in your group, or ponder them on your own.

- What did Peter and John do when Mary Magdalene told them that the tomb was empty? What did they see when they got there? What was the Beloved Disciple's response to what they saw?
- What do you think you would have done if you had been at the tomb with Peter, Mary, and the Beloved Disciple? Why?

Read John 21:21–24; then discuss these questions in your group, or ponder them on your own.

- How does the Beloved Disciple remain until Jesus comes? What is one way in which Jesus might be calling you to witness about Him to others?
- Seeing the example of the Beloved Disciple remaining at the cross, believing in the Resurrection, and witnessing to the world, how do you feel? How can the other people in your Bible study (or your other friends) pray for you?

Conclusion

As we come to the end of our Bible study, I hope you have learned and grown as much as I did when I went through my own transformative journey into discipleship. Let me tell you a little bit about my journey.

At twenty-five, I was a seminarian for the Diocese of Houma-Thibodaux in Louisiana, which I currently serve as a priest. My bishop had asked me to prepare for postgraduate studies in Sacred Scripture; I had just completed the *Spiritual Exercises*; and my diocese was in the early days of a massive strategic-planning initiative. One evening I was invited to the first meeting of the preparatory commission for this strategic plan, and I heard words that made my heart sink: "We can no longer say that South Louisiana is Catholic." In the forty years of the existence of our little diocese, we had lost one-third of our Catholics.[83] What were we going to do?

Throughout my life I had seen the loss with my own eyes. From year to year the pews around me were filled with fewer and fewer people. It broke my heart. I had begun to know the real joy that came from relationship with Jesus. I had experienced His consolations in prayer. I had known His presence sustaining me in the difficulties of

---

83. In 1977, when the diocese was founded, our area was 67 percent Catholic, and as we approached our fortieth anniversary in 2017, we were only 38 percent Catholic.

life. I knew beyond doubt that relationship with Jesus was the only
way to ultimate meaning in the days of this life and into the eternity
of heaven. It broke my heart that my friends were going away from
the liturgy, where heaven meets earth, away from the Eucharist, and
away from the deep mercy of God in Reconciliation.

I was ready to commit my life to helping people live the fullness
of joy that Jesus offers in His Church. But how would I accomplish
the mission God was entrusting to me with things being the way they
were? We must, our bishop said, go back to the original mission of the
Church, the mission given to her by Jesus Himself: "Go therefore and
make disciples of all nations, baptizing them in the name of the Father
and of the Son and of the Holy Spirit, teaching them to observe all
that I have commanded you" (Matthew 28:19–20a, emphases added).
This life in relationship with Jesus that I had begun to live is called
discipleship. It seemed to me that the reason people were leaving the
Church might be because we were not effectively showing them how
to be disciples of Jesus. They were leaving because although their
bodies might be physically present in the pews on Sunday because it
was "the right thing to do," many had not encountered Jesus in their
hearts, nor had they truly begun to believe in Him. They were losing
faith in the Eucharist, which, as we have seen, Jesus gives us to deepen
and continue our discipleship. We needed to accompany our people
on the path of discipleship. We needed to refocus on the mission that
Jesus has left to us.

With passionate conviction in my heart, I read everything I could
on discipleship.[84] But I was not satisfied with what I found. Some of

---

84. Of particular note are the insightful works of Sherry Weddell, *Forming Intentional
    Disciples: The Path to Knowing and Following Jesus* (Huntington, IN: Our Sunday
    Visitor, 2012) and Thom S. Rainer and Eric Geiger, *Simple Church: Returning to God's
    Process for Making Disciples* (Nashville, TN: B&H Publishing, 2011). There are
    websites such as www.discipleship.org and parish evangelization programs such as the
    Augustine Institute's *YDisciple*. Of greatest impact in the United States today may be

the works I read are excellent, but they are structured upon experience rather than how the Bible presents this concept of discipleship. Their method is legitimate, and most of the conclusions they come to are correct, but without a deep dive into what the Scriptures themselves explicitly reveal about discipleship, two consequences are likely to occur. The first and most dangerous is that we could easily depart from God's revelation into mere human thinking. The second consequence is that we will almost certainly miss some of the depths of understanding and fullness of living discipleship offered by God to the church. And finally, I felt that works that are not rooted in Scripture did not probe deeply enough into the matter.

My bishop wanted me to study the Bible. He also wanted our people to live as disciples. And I had an opportunity to take a deep dive into exactly what the Bible says about being a disciple of Jesus. The last two years of seminary were meant to be a time of integration, and I found an expression of that integration in writing my master's thesis on the topic of "Discipleship in the Bible." With prayer and clear discernment that this was God's will, I dove headlong into this study.

After a year or two of research, work, lots of prayer, and almost as much coffee, I completed the thesis, finished seminary, and was ordained a priest. I went from the classroom to the mission field and from studying about the making of disciples to actual, full-time engagement in the mission. I've preached on discipleship, I have given talks on the topic, and I have designed plans that are being implemented to form disciples in parishes. I've walked one-on-one with disciples in day-to-day work, in spiritual direction, and in hearing confessions. Repeatedly, I've used in the field what I learned over

---

the excellent and largely successful discipleship-centered ministry of the Fellowship of Catholic University Students (FOCUS), the method for which was outlined by founder Curtis Martin in *Making Missionary Disciples: How to Live the Method Modeled by the Master* (Genesee, CO: FOCUS, 2018).

those many days I spent with my nose in the books. I've also kept thinking that it could be helpful for other pastors, preachers, and spiritual directors, along with any Christian trying to grow in relationship with Jesus, to have this same knowledge of what the Bible really means by discipleship at their fingertips.

This is the knowledge you are holding in your hands. This book explains precisely what the Gospel of John teaches about what it means to be a disciple, and gives clear and practical ways for you to apply that teaching of the Lord in your life as well as in the lives of those you accompany on your journey with Jesus.

My prayer for you is that having now read and prayed with this book, you seek to remain with Jesus as did Andrew, that you bring others to Him as did Philip, and that you are patient with your own growth in discipleship, uneven as it may be, as you observe how even the first disciples stumbled along their way. I hope that you believe with the fervor of the Samaritans and persevere with the tenacity of the man born blind. May you bear abundant fruit as you journey to the "remaining place" prepared for you by Jesus and, like the Beloved Disciple, give lasting witness to the redeeming love God has for us!

Following the example of the disciples who have come before us and whose witness is recorded in the Gospel of John, may we, too, believe and remain in Jesus, becoming true disciples as we enter into the union of the Father, Son, and Holy Spirit forever!

For Your Small Group

Practical Tips

How to Lead a Small Group

With gratitude to Maegan Martin for drafting this section.

So, you're committed to Going Deeper in your discipleship, and you're going to get a few friends together to do this Bible study. But maybe you've never led a Bible study before. Maybe you've never been to one. How do you do this? What's Bible study supposed to look like?

Don't worry. Trust in Jesus and follow these instructions.

First, your job as a small-group leader is *not* necessarily to teach, to know all the answers, or to be the theologian in the room. Your role in leading the Bible study is simply to facilitate a conversation that leads to an encounter with Jesus Christ in the words that He left us. To do that, it's important to prepare for Bible study.

Preparation

Taking the time to read through the chapter being discussed, the Scripture passages that are being studied, and the questions at the end of each chapter *in advance* can lead to a more fruitful conversation during your small group. You know the people in your small group best. Preparing for the small-group discussion will allow you to focus on the questions you know will mean the most to your group and understand where the conversation should be going. Take time to sit before the Lord with the materials. This will also allow you to share from your own experience in prayer with the Scripture. There's no need to try to use every question in the book. Ask Jesus for guidance, and choose the ones that you think will best serve the unique identity of your group. Sometimes you may use them all, and sometimes you may use only a couple. Sometimes you may even use different questions that come to you in prayer. In other words, do whatever facilitates a natural, meaningful, fruitful dialogue about the Lord and His word.

Tools and Skills

1. Again, your role is not to teach but to facilitate an encounter—with Jesus and with the members of your group. Asking good questions is important. While the main questions are provided for you, you may want to ask a few more to keep the conversation going. When you prepare for the small group, write down questions that you have while reading through the chapter and the Scripture passages. When someone in the group asks a question, let other members of the group answer. This will help you facilitate a conversation rather than deliver a lecture.

2. There may be times your group will need a little direction. As a small-group leader, your job is to encourage and direct the members of your group through the Bible study. When someone shares, it's important to affirm their willingness to participate, even if the answer isn't spot on. Good direction in a small group will help ensure that your group understands all the main points of the study. This could look like gently redirecting the group back on topic after a tangent, using your body language to encourage some of the less talkative members of your group to share, or going deeper into a particular topic that is both relevant to the study and important to your group.

That's it. Leading a small group *is* something that we can continue to grow in, but it's *not* something that takes a master's degree or months of training. Love the people in your group, trust Jesus, ask questions, and pray. It's going to be great!

Going Deeper Possible Answers

Chapter 1: Discipleship in the Bible, pages 3–12

The Main Thing: Being introduced to the Bible's concept of discipleship, we want to (1) learn, in brief, what makes a true disciple of Jesus and (2) start off on the right foot, opening our hearts to Jesus for this study.

- Where do you find yourself as we begin our journey together? What do you want out of this Bible study? What do you think when you hear the word *disciple* right now?

- In which books of the New Testament is the word *disciple* used? Which book has the word *disciple* the most? According to this chapter, what does this tell us about the use of the word *disciple* in the time of Jesus?

- **Answer:** The word *disciple* is used in the Gospels and in the Acts of the Apostles. St. John's Gospel has it the most—seventy-eight times. The fact that *disciple* is used only in the books that tell the true story of the life of Jesus (the Gospels) and how His ministry continued through His Church (Acts) suggests that *disciple* is the word that Jesus Himself used to describe His followers.

Read John 8:31; then discuss these questions in your group, or ponder them on your own.

- According to John 8:31, what are the two central things that a true disciple does? What do you think when you hear the word *believe* right now? The word *remain*?

- **Answer:** A disciple *believes and remains in Jesus.*

- According to pages 8–9, what are the four basic dynamics of a person's growth in discipleship? How does this describe your experience of discipleship?

- **Answer:** (1) Someone *witnesses* to me about Jesus, giving the first spark of belief; (2) I have a *personal encounter with Jesus*, which solidifies the belief; (3) I chose to *remain with Jesus*, even through trials, temptations, and sufferings; and (4) empowered by the Holy Spirit, my *believing and remaining bear fruit in practical love.*

- What are you most excited about as we begin to learn about discipleship together? How can the other people in your Bible study (or your other friends) pray for you?

Chapter 2: The Disciples Meet Jesus, pages 15–24

The Main Thing: Reflecting on the call of the first disciples, we want to (1) come to a practical idea of how to remain with Jesus and (2) hope that remaining with Him is possible for us.

- Where do you find yourself as a disciple today? Has anything changed since you started this book?

Read John 1:35–46; then discuss these questions in your group, or ponder them on your own.

- Who introduced you to Jesus? Who was your John the Baptist, Andrew, or Philip? How did they do it?
- **Possible Answers:**

  ○ They invited me to Adoration.

  ○ They were willing to talk through all of my questions about the faith.

  ○ They were there for me during a very hard time in my life.

- What did Andrew and the other disciple do when they met Jesus? Why do you think this is important?
- **Answer:** They stayed [Greek: *remained*] with Him for the rest of that day (John 1:39).
- What else did Andrew do as a result of meeting Jesus? Can you see yourself in Andrew's place in the story? What does that look like to you?
- **Answer:** He (1) found his brother Simon to tell him about Jesus and (2) brought him to Jesus (John 1:41–42).
- What are the two steps of Nathanael's first encounter with Jesus? Why do you think each of these steps is important?
- **Answer:** (1) He listens to Philip's witness (albeit with skepticism) (John 1:45–46); then (2) he meets Jesus for himself (John 1:41–42).
- In John 1, what is Jesus teaching us about discipleship?
- **Possible Answers:**
  - The main thing that a disciple does is live (*remain*) in relationship with Jesus Christ (John 1:35–39).
  - Disciples desire to bring others to meet Jesus, too (John 1:40–42; 43–46).

Reread the quote from Pope St. John Paul II on page 22.

- What are some ways that our culture "dreams of happiness"? What are one or two hopes and desires of people in the world today that can be points of contact with the Gospel?

Remember Megan's story from pages 18–19:

- She remained with Jesus through Eucharistic Adoration, diving into the Scriptures, and approaching the sacraments. Does this sound like a life that you want to live? What are the roadblocks to living this life? Which one of these three (Adoration, Scripture, sacraments) can you engage with this week? Who will keep you accountable to making the effort to remain with Jesus?

Megan used her platform as an athlete to share her faith. What platforms do you have? Who listens to you? Whom can you gently and clearly introduce to Jesus? And how? Who will keep you accountable to actively witnessing your faith to others?

(**Note:** Digital platforms are fine, but think, too, about more personal opportunities to gently and naturally talk about Jesus.)

- After walking through the true story of the call of the first disciples, how do you feel? How can the other people in your Bible study (or your other friends) pray for you?

Chapter 3: Discipleship Is a Process, pages 25–31

The Main Thing: Reflecting on how the first disciples began to *grow* in their discipleship, we want to (1) understand that one doesn't become a disciple in a moment and it is normal to progress slowly on the path of discipleship and (2) see more clearly what it means to believe in Jesus.

- Where do you find yourself as a disciple today? Has anything changed since you started this book?

Read John 2:1–11; then discuss these questions in your group, or ponder them on your own.

- What miracle did Jesus perform at the wedding in Cana? What did it signify? Especially in light of Philip's conversation with Nathanael, explored in chapter 2 of this book, why do you think this particular miracle may be important?
- **Answer:** He turned water into wine. Old Testament prophecies indicate that the presence of abundant wine points to the fact

that Jesus is the Messiah. Jesus is proving Himself to be the one of whom Moses and the prophets had written.

- Do you believe in Jesus?

    ○ If so, what were some of the first things that began to convince you? Maybe it was the witness of another person. Maybe it was a miracle, a big blessing, or a powerful emotional experience.

    ○ If not, what are you looking for? What do you think might move you to both believe and work to remain?

- What new things have you learned about discipleship in John 2?

- **Possible Answers:**

    ○ We saw more clearly that being a disciple isn't just a one-time thing but a process in relationship.

    ○ We saw how, to be a disciple, believing is just as important as remaining.

Read John 2:11–12 and 23–25; then discuss these questions in your group, or ponder them on your own.

- What's the difference between the disciples' response to Jesus and the response of the people in Jerusalem? Based upon your reading of this chapter, why might it be that their responses were different?

- **Possible Answers:**

    ○ The disciples remained with Him, but Jesus did not choose to remain with the people in Jerusalem.

    ○ The disciples' remaining with Him shows that their belief was more than mere signs faith, but the people in Jerusalem were focused only on the sign.

○ The disciples were beginning to believe in Jesus, growing in relationship with Him, but the people in Jerusalem were not open to this relationship.

- The people in Jerusalem could not enter into a trusting relationship with Jesus. Are there places in your life where you struggle to trust Jesus? What or who might be able to help you trust Jesus more in one of these places?

- Have you ever experienced a miracle? Powerful emotional experiences with Jesus? What did you learn from those experiences? How did you or did you not allow the miracle(s) or the emotional experience(s) to lead you deeper into relationship with Jesus?

- After walking with the first disciples as they begin to grow in their discipleship, how do you feel? What's in your mind and heart regarding Jesus today? How can the other people in your Bible study (or your other friends) pray for you?

Chapter 4: *Believe* like a Samaritan, pages 35–44

The Main Thing: Seeing St. Photina come to believe in Jesus through her personal encounter with Him, we want to (1) *encounter* Him ourselves and (2) *witness* to Him as passionate disciples.

- Where do you find yourself as a disciple today? Has anything changed since you started this book?

Remember the history of the hatred between the Jews and the Samaritans (pages 35–36).

- What does Jesus' inviting Samaritans into discipleship teach us about discipleship? Does this invitation make you think of any certain person whom Jesus might be calling you to reach out to in your own life?

- **Possible Answer:**

  - Jesus' invitation to discipleship is not limited to a certain race or to a privileged few but even extended to those whom we might wrongly think are unworthy.

Read John 4:39–42; then discuss these questions in your group, or ponder them on your own.

- What did the Samaritans do after they heard the woman's witness? What might have made them ready to do that?
- **Answers:**

  - They began to believe in Jesus (John 4:39).
  - They asked Jesus to remain with them (John 4:40).

- What was the result of Jesus' encounter with the Samaritans as He remained with them?
- Why do you think they might have responded in these ways?
- **Answers:**

  - "Many more believed because of his word" (John 4:41).
  - They came to know that is He is the Savior of the world (John 4:42).

Read John 4:7–30; then discuss these questions in your group, or ponder them on your own.

- St. Photina's own story, even the sinful parts, was a part of her witness. "Come, see a man who told me all that I ever did" (John 4:29a). How do you think it might have felt for her to share her faith when everyone in the town knew her sin? Using the virtues of prudence and of courage, how might Jesus be asking you to share parts of your story with others in witness to Him?

Prudence is knowing the right thing to do in the particular situations in which we find ourselves.
Courage is perseverance in doing that right thing, especially over time or in the midst of obstacles.

- St. Photina had to encounter Jesus personally to begin a relationship with Him. The other Samaritans began to believe because of her witness, but they also had to encounter Jesus and believe for themselves. Do you encounter Jesus regularly in your life? If not, where might be a good place to start?

- After walking through the true story of St. Photina and her fellow Samaritans, how do you feel? How can the other people in your Bible study (or your other friends) pray for you?

Chapter 5: Work to *Remain*, pages 45–52

The Main Thing: Listening to Jesus' teaching in John 6, we want to work to remain in Him by (1) learning from Him and (2) receiving the gift of His Flesh and Blood.

- Where do you find yourself as a disciple today? Has anything changed since you started this book?

Read John 6:25–34; then discuss these questions in your group, or ponder them on your own.

- Why does the crowd cross the sea in search of Jesus? What is the work that Jesus wants them to do?

- **Answer:** They want bread to satisfy their hunger (John 6:26, 34), but Jesus invites them into the work of *believing* in Him and receiving the gift of *remaining* into eternal life (John 6:27, 29).

- The crowd following Jesus seems to be in it for the freebies. What are you in it for? Why do you come to relationship with

Jesus? Remembering that each one of us on this side of heaven has some mixed motivations—some desire for the "free-bies"—how, if at all, do you want your motivations to grow and change?

Read John 6:40–47; then discuss these questions in your group, or ponder them on your own.

- What is the will of the Father? Do you believe what Jesus says in John 6:40? What are some of the obstacles to believing this revelation—for yourself and/or for others?

- **Answer:** Jesus says, *"For this is the will of my Father, that every one who sees the Son* and believes in him should have eternal life; and I will raise him up at the last day"* (John 6:40, emphasis added).

- **Possible Answer:** Sometimes past hurts or our own failures in the battle for virtue convince us that Jesus is an impartial observer or an implacable judge. Sometimes we get convinced that He's not on our side (which is a lie), so we either begin to despair or try to prove ourselves to Him. The solution is to remember His promises and to choose to trust by acting upon His promises, even when we don't feel very much confidence. Start small and slowly build up to greater trust.

- What do the Jews in this scene do when Jesus reveals the will of the Father? How, in your life, do you act similarly? What is one thing that you can do this week that would help you have a little more trust in Jesus?

- **Answer:** They murmur at Him and make excuses as to why they should not believe what He says.

- **Note:** While God desires every human being to become a disciple of Jesus, His rejection by some Jews in the past gives no excuse for hatred or discrimination at any time or in any circumstance.

- A disciple learns from Jesus—from God. What are some good ways to learn from and about our Lord?

Read John 6:52–59 and the Catechism of the Catholic Church, §1335–1336 and 1410–1419; then discuss these questions in your group, or ponder them on your own.

- In John 6, what does Jesus say that we must do to remain in Him and for Him to remain in us? According to Jesus, is consuming His Body and Blood necessary for life? What implications does this have for our lives?
- **Answer:** We must eat His Flesh and drink His Blood (John 6:56), which is necessary for life (John 6:53). We should receive the Eucharist in a state of grace at Mass as often as we can.

Read John 6:66–71 and John 13:21–30; then discuss these questions in your group, or ponder them on your own.

- Where is your faith most vulnerable? Which is the hardest teaching revealed by God for you to believe? What is one thing you can do this week to learn more and strengthen your faith?
- **Possible Answers:** First, always ask God for understanding. It is very good to go to Mass, receiving Jesus' Flesh and Blood with the intention of greater faith and understanding. It is very good to go to Eucharistic Adoration, resting in the real presence of Jesus with the intention of greater faith and understanding. It is also very important to do the work of study. Read the *Catechism of the Catholic Church* on the topic you're struggling with (the index in the back of the *Catechism* includes a list of all the topics that are covered). You can make an appointment with your priest to talk it out. If you make the appointment, tell him or

his secretary, "I'd like to have thirty minutes (or however much time you think you'll need) to talk about _____," so that he can be prepared to serve you well.

- After learning about the work of remaining and the importance of receiving the Body and Blood of Jesus for discipleship, how do you feel? How can the other people in your Bible study (or your other friends) pray for you?

Chapter 6: *Perseverance* leads to *Devotion*, pages 53–63

The Main Thing: Through the teaching of Jesus and the example of the man born blind, we see that (1) remaining in Jesus often looks like continuing to believe in the midst of suffering, and (2) this perseverance naturally leads to devotion. I will worship the God whom I have come to know in the storm.

- Where do you find yourself as a disciple today? Has anything changed since you started this book?

Read John 9:6–12; then discuss these questions in your group, or ponder them on your own.

- What does Jesus do to heal the man of his blindness? What is the significance of these two actions?
- **Answer:** Jesus rubs clay into his eyes and then sends the man to wash in the pool of Siloam. The clay reminds us of the creation of humanity in Genesis 2:7, and the washing in the pool reminds us of baptism.
- What does the word *Siloam* mean? Why is this significant? Does this have any implications for your life?
- **Answer:** *Siloam* means "sent." Jesus' instruction that the blind man wash in a pool named "Sent" shows us that all of the

baptized, even brand-new, novice disciples, are sent by Jesus to bear witness to Him.

Read John 9:24–34; then discuss these questions in your group, or ponder them on your own.

- What do the Pharisees eventually do to the man? Why do they do this?
- **Answer:** "They cast him out" (John 9:34).
- The Pharisees challenged the man's faith. What are common challenges to a person's faith today? Which ones affect you? Is it hard or easy to call yourself a disciple of Jesus in public? What makes it so?
- Even before he believed in Jesus, the formerly blind man believed in the works performed by Jesus, and this belief sustained him in his trials. What are a few works, both small and large, that Jesus has done in your life?

Read John 9:35–41; then discuss these questions in your group, or ponder them on your own.

- What does Jesus do when he hears that the Pharisees have cast out the formerly blind man? Has there ever been a time when you've felt particularly close to Jesus after a time of difficult struggles?
- **Answer:** Jesus finds him and tells him that He is the Messiah (John 9:35–38).
- What does the formerly blind man do when Jesus tells him that He is the Messiah? How could you respond to Jesus more like this model disciple? What are your biggest obstacles?
- **Answer:** He calls Jesus "Lord," confesses "I believe," and "worships" Jesus (John 9:38).

- After walking through the true story of the man born blind, how do you feel? How can the other people in your Bible study (or your other friends) pray for you?

Chapter 7: *Love* One Another, pages 65–73

The Main Thing: Hearing Jesus' words to His disciples, we learn that (1) to remain is to be at home in the family of God, now and forever, as friends of Jesus and (2) this relationship bears fruit in practical love.

- Where do you find yourself as a disciple today? Has anything changed since you started this book?

Read John 14:1–4; then discuss these questions in your group, or ponder them on your own.

- At the beginning of John 14, what does Jesus ask His disciples to do? What are some common obstacles to doing that? What are the most common obstacles for you?
- **Answer:** To believe or trust in Him (John 14:1)
- What thoughts and emotions stir in your mind and heart as you think of Jesus preparing a place for you in heaven?

Read 1 John 3:23–24, then discuss these questions in your group, or ponder them on your own.

- What ways are you, as a disciple, naturally inclined to express love for others (examples: intercessory prayer, service to the poor, teaching others, pro-life work, etc.)? Are there any ways where God might be calling you to grow, for example, in different expressions of love or maybe with greater dedication or intensity in the ways in which you are naturally inclined?

Read John 15:1–17; then discuss these questions in your group, or ponder them on your own.

- What does the Father do for the branch that bears fruit? Why does He do this? What might this look like in the life of a disciple?
- **Answer:** He prunes it, so that it may bear more fruit (John 15:2).
- What can a disciple do apart from Jesus? What happens with a disciple who remains in Jesus? Have you seen a difference in your life between being apart from Jesus and remaining in Him? What was the difference?
- **Answer:** Apart from Jesus, we can do nothing, and the disciple who remains in Jesus bears much fruit. (John 15:5).
- According to this chapter, what are the two big-picture ways in which disciples bear fruit? What are one or two practical ways in which you can focus on each of these ways of fruit bearing?
- **Answer:** (1) Building up fellow disciples inside the Church and (2) witnessing to others so as to invite them into this family.
- After learning about the "remaining place" prepared for you by Jesus, being invited to remain united to Him as His friend, and hearing Jesus' image of the vine and the branches, how do you feel? How can the other people in your Bible study (or your other friends) pray for you?

Chapter 8: The Beloved Disciple, pages 75–82

The Main Thing: Seeing the example of the Beloved Disciple, we hope to imitate him in (1) belief, even when it's imperfect; (2) remaining, especially through the crosses that enter our lives; and (3) the loving action of witnessing to others about Jesus.

- Where do you find yourself as a disciple today? Has anything changed since you started this book?

Read John 19:25–37. Let yourself feel the emotion of the scene. Imagine yourself there with Jesus and Mary and the Beloved Disciple. Then discuss these questions in your group, or ponder them on your own.

- What thoughts and emotions come up as you look upon Jesus crucified? How might Jesus be calling you to bear witness to this love of His in the world?
- What is your relationship with Mary like? Are there any struggles in that relationship? How could you open your heart a little more to heed the Gospel's invitation to take her into your own?

Read John 20:1–10; then discuss these questions in your group, or ponder them on your own.

- What did Peter and John do when Mary Magdalene told them that the tomb was empty? What did they see when they got there? What is the Beloved Disciple's response to what they saw?
- **Answer:** (1) They ran to the tomb. (2) Getting there, they saw a tomb that was empty but tidy, not the way robbers would have left it. (3) The Beloved Disciple "saw and believed" or, perhaps better, "began to believe" (John 20:8–10).
- What do you think you would have done if you had been there with Peter, Mary, and the Beloved Disciple? Why?

Read John 21:21–24; then discuss these questions in your group, or ponder them on your own.

- How does the Beloved Disciple remain until Jesus comes? What is one way in which Jesus might be calling you to witness about Him to others?
- **Possible Answer:** The Beloved Disciple's witness, which he wrote down to record as this Gospel, continues to foster faith in new disciples throughout the centuries.

- Seeing the example of the Beloved Disciple remaining at the cross, believing in the Resurrection, and witnessing to the world, how do you feel? How can the other people in your Bible study (or your other friends) pray for you?

Bibliography

Augustine. "Tractates on the Gospel According to St. John." In *Nicene and Post-Nicene Fathers*. Edited by Philip Schaff. New York: Christian Literature Company, 1889.

Barrett, Charles Kingsley. *The Gospel according to St. John: An Introduction with Commentary and Notes on the Greek Text*. 2nd ed. Philadelphia: Westminster Press, 1978.

Beasley-Murray, George R. *John*. *Word Biblical Commentary*. Nashville: Thomas Nelson, 1999.

Benedict XIV. *The Roman Martyrology*. Translated by the Archbishop of Baltimore. Baltimore: John Murphy and Co., 1916.

Brown, Raymond E. *An Introduction to the Gospel of John*. Edited by Francis J. Moloney. New York: Doubleday, 2003.

———. *The Gospel according to John*. 2 vols. The Anchor Yale Bible. New Haven, CT: Yale University Press, 1966.

Bultmann, Rudolf. *The Gospel of John: A Commentary*. Translated by G. R. Beasley-Murray. Oxford: Basil Blackwell, 1971.

Catechism of the Catholic Church. 2nd ed. Vatican City: Libreria Editrice Vaticana, 1994.

Chrysostom, John. "Homilies on the Gospel of St. John." In *Nicene and Post-Nicene Fathers*. Edited by Philip Schaff. New York: Christian Literature Company, 1889.

————. In *Ancient Christian Commentary on Scripture: New Testament*, Vol. IVa, *John 1—10*. Edited by Joel C. Elowsky. Downers Grove, IL: InterVarsity Press, 2006.

Cyril of Alexandria. *Commentary on the Gospel of John*. In *Ancient Christian Commentary on Scripture: New Testament*, Vol. IVA. *John 1—10*. Edited by Joel C. Elowsky. Downers Grove, IL: InterVarsity Press, 2006.

Danker, Frederick W., Walter Bauer, William F. Arndt, and F. Wilbur Gingrich. *Greek-English Lexicon of the New Testament and Other Early Christian Literature*. 3rd ed. Chicago: University of Chicago Press, 2000.

De Jonge, Marinus. *Jesus: Stranger from Heaven and Son of God*. Missoula, MT: Scholars Press, 1977.

Francis. *Evangelii Gaudium*. "Apostolic Exhortation on the Proclamation of the Gospel in Today's World." November 24, 2013. http://w2.vatican.va/content/francesco/en/apost_exhortations/documents/papa-francesco_esortazione-ap_20131124_evangelii-gaudium.

————. *Lumen Fidei*. Encyclical Letter. June 29 2013. http://www.vatican.va/content/francesco/en/encyclicals/documents/papa-francesco_20130629_enciclica-lumen-fidei.html.

Glimm, Francis X., trans. *Didache*. In *The Fathers of the Church: A New Translation*, Vol. 1. *The Apostolic Fathers*. Washington, DC: Catholic University of America Press, 1947.

Gregory, Brad. *The Unintended Reformation: How a Religious Revolution Secularized Society*. Cambridge, MA: Belknap Press/Harvard University Press, 2012.

Hahn, Scott. *Catholic Bible Dictionary*. New York: Doubleday, 2009.

————. "Temple, Sign, and Sacrament: Towards a New Perspective on the Gospel of John." *Letter and Spirit* 4 (2008): 107–143.

Hillmer, Melvyn R. "They Believed in Him: Discipleship in the Johannine Tradition." In *Patterns of Discipleship in the New Testament*. Edited by Richard N. Longenecker. Grand Rapids, MI: Eerdmans, 1996.

John Paul II. Address at the Prayer Vigil for the Fifteenth World Youth Day, Rome. August 19, 2000. http://w2.vatican.va/content/john-paul-ii/en/speeches/2000/jul-sep/documents/hf_jp-ii_spe_20000819_gmg-veglia.html.

———. Encyclical Letter, *Redemptoris Mater* (25 March 1987). http://w2.vatican.va/content/john-paul-ii/en/encyclicals/documents/hf_jp-ii_enc_25031987_redemptoris-mater.html.

———. Homily for the Solemnity of Mary, Mother of God (1 January 1997). http://www.vatican.va/content/john-paul-ii/en/homilies/1997/documents/hf_jp-ii_hom_19970101.html.

Justin Martyr. *First Apology*. Translated by Thomas B. Falls. In *The Fathers of the Church: A New Translation: Saint Justin Martyr*. Washington, DC: Catholic University of America Press, 1948.

Keener, Craig S. *The Gospel of John: A Commentary*. 2 vols. Grand Rapids, MI: Baker Academic, 2003.

Kreeft, Peter. "The Argument from Pascal's Wager." http://www.peterkreeft.com/topics/pascals-wager.htm.

Lewis, Clive Staples. *Mere Christianity*. London: Collins, 1952.

Martin, Francis and Wright, William M. IV. *The Gospel of John Catholic Commentary on Sacred Scripture*. Grand Rapids, MI: Baker Academic, 2015.

Meier, John P. *Companions and Competitors*. Vol. 3 of *A Marginal Jew, Rethinking the Historical Jesus*. New Haven/London: Yale University Press, 2001.

Painter, John. *John: Witness and Theologian*. London: SPCK, 1975.

Paschal, Blaise. "Pensées." In *Modern Philosophy*. Translated by W. F. Trotter. Vol. 3 of *Philosophic Classics*. Edited by Forrest E. Baird and Walter Kaufmann. New York: Prentice Hall, 1996.

Pitre, Brant. *The Case for Jesus: The Biblical and Historical Evidence for Christ*. New York: Image, 2016.

————. *Jesus the Bridegroom: The Greatest Love Story Ever Told*. New York: Image, 2014.

Schnackenburg, Rudolf. *The Gospel according to St. John*. Translated by Kevin Smyth. Vol. 1 of *Herder's Theological Commentary on the New Testament*. New York: Herder and Herder, 1968.

————. *The Gospel according to St. John*. Translated by Cecily Hastings, Francis McDonagh, David Smith, and Richard Foley. Vol. 2 of *Herder's Theological Commentary on the New Testament*. New York: Crossroad, 1980.

————. *The Gospel according to St. John*. Translated by David Smith and G. A. Kon. Vol. 3 of *Herder's Theological Commentary on the New Testament*. New York: Crossroad, 1982.

Segovia, Fernando F. "Peace I Leave with You; My Peace I Give to You: Discipleship in the Fourth Gospel." In *Discipleship in the New Testament*. Edited by Fernando F. Segovia. Philadelphia: Fortress, 1985.

Smith, Robert H. "Seeking Jesus in the Gospel of John." *Currents in Theology and Mission* 15:1 (1988).

Wilkins, Michael J. "Disciples and Discipleship." In *Dictionary of Jesus and the Gospels: A Compendium of Contemporary Biblical Scholarship*. Edited by Joel B. Green, Jeannine K. Brown, and Nicholas Perrin. 2nd ed. Downers Grove, IL: IVP Academic, 2013.

————. *Following the Master: A Biblical Theology of Discipleship*. Grand Rapids: Zondervan, 1992.

Acknowledgments

What a gift it is to be able to write a book explaining a small piece of the written word of God! I am most grateful to the Lord for this gift as I also offer thanks to the many men and women who graciously played a part in this project. First, I am most grateful to Dr. Brant Pitre, who directed my 2017 master's thesis, for which I conducted the research that informed this book and who, three years later, suggested that I reach out to Loyola Press as the right publisher for this book. I am also grateful to Father Mark Thibodeaux, SJ, who helped me discern that it was, in fact, the voice of God inviting me to write this book at this time, in contrast to being prompted merely by my own personal desires. Father Mark also kindly introduced me to Gary Jansen at Loyola Press, without whom this project may not have happened.

I am also grateful to Gary and the team at Loyola. Gary's excellent editing, Christian kindness, and endless patience were a blessed gift to this new author. It is thanks to Gary that this book is readable and relatable.

I wrote this book during my final six months as pastor of Holy Cross Parish in Morgan City, Louisiana, as well as during my first year studying Scripture at the Pontifical Biblical Institute. The gracious way my parishioners received my first book, *Daily Lessons from the Saints* (Emeryville, CA: Rockridge Press, 2020), and their continued encouragement were real factors in my discernment to write this one. But—the responsibilities of a pastor being what they are—there is no way that I could have completed it without the incredibly hard work of my staff and many volunteers. I am especially grateful to Maegan, Mary, Father Brett, and Father Patrick for their close collaboration in the pastoral care of the people of God in Morgan City during the time I devoted to writing.

To each of you who read all or part of the manuscript and offered your observations, encouragements, and constructive criticisms, I am deeply grateful.

Special thanks go to Jennifer Ely, who has read more versions of this manuscript than I can count, offering insight, encouragement, and support all along the way; to Maegan Martin, the best Bible study leader and Bible study writer I know, who provided extensive help in making this book into a usable Bible study for any home, parish, or group of friends; and to Jessica Harvey, who contributed her personal experience at forming disciples in a parish and her professional expertise in English grammar to the work, reading the entire manuscript twice!

Finally, many thanks to my parents, who always give me their support. I am grateful for many phone calls with my momma, bringing much stress relief. And when days were long and the writing was hard, I often remembered the words of my daddy after I finished my first book: "I knew you'd write books." This confidence from my dad strengthened me and moved me forward!

> O give thanks to the LORD, for he is good;
> for his [mercy] endures for ever! (Psalm 107:1)

Rome, Italy
January 6, 2022
The Epiphany of the Lord

About the Author

Father S. Brice Higginbotham is a Catholic priest for the Diocese of Houma-Thibodaux in Louisiana who is currently pursuing a Licentiate in Sacred Scripture at the Pontifical Biblical Institute in Rome, Italy. Ordained to the priesthood of Jesus Christ in 2017, Father Brice has previously served as pastor of Holy Cross Parish, Chaplain of Central Catholic School, *censor librorum*, consultant to the Office of Parish Support, master of ceremonies, parochial vicar at Christ the Redeemer Parish and the Cathedral of St. Francis de Sales, assistant vocations director, state police chaplain, and member of the diocesan presbyteral council.

Father Brice received his master's degree in theological studies from Notre Dame Seminary in New Orleans, Louisiana. He has published one other book, *Daily Lessons from the Saints* (Rockridge Press, 2020), articles and homilies in *Homiletic & Pastoral Review*, and more than sixty catechetical videos in cooperation with the Diocese of Houma-Thibodaux's Offices of Parish Support and Communications, all of which are available on YouTube and Facebook.

A special preview of Father Brice Higginbotham's

DAILY LESSONS FROM THE

SAINTS

52 WEEKS OF INSPIRATION
AND ENCOURAGEMENT

FATHER BRICE HIGGENBOTHAM

ROCKRIDGE
PRESS

WEEK 1
Mary, Queen of All Saints

Mother of God, Queen of All Saints

Mother of All Peoples

FEAST DAY: Multiple, but January 1 is the Feast (Solemnity) of Mary, Mother of God, her most fundamental title.

DAY 1

On the heels of Christmas, we continue to reflect on the manger scene, in which we encounter not just the child Jesus but also Mary, Joseph, the animals, the shepherds, and, after a while, even the wise men. Jesus is obviously the most important person in the manger scene, but who is the second most important person there? Mary, His mother!

† We all have many memories of Christmas—memories of family, food, presents, and the rest. When you think of Christmas, what makes you think of Jesus? Spend a few moments today thanking God for that memory.

DAY 2

Why do we love Mary so much? Why do we Catholics give her so much honor? The answer is this: Imagine you had the opportunity to create your own mother. Imagine how you would make her. Imagine how much you would want to preserve her from anything bad, from anything evil, from anything wicked. That is Mary.

† Think about your mother today. How has her life blessed you? Where does she need your prayers? Offer a prayer to God today for your mother.

DAY 3

We honor Mary because she is the Mother of God. We honor Mary because Jesus honors Mary in creating her. Everything we believe about Mary comes from the fundamental truth that she is the Mother of God the Son and that she is therefore the mother of us—everything we believe about Mary is based on or protects that which we believe about Jesus.

† Open your Bible to Matthew 1:18–2:23. What do you think it was like for Mary and Joseph to talk about this baby having been conceived miraculously? To receive the visit of the wise men, to fly by night into Egypt, to return to Nazareth? Imagine yourself in one of these scenes. What might God be teaching you through this scene?

DAY 4

In the Bible, St. Paul remembers St. Timothy's sincere faith, "a faith that dwelt first in your grandmother Lois and your mother Eunice and now, I am sure, dwells in you" (2 Timothy 1:5). Like Lois and Eunice mothered Timothy, Mary must surely have prayed with Jesus and remembered the Scriptures with Him.

† Who do you consider a spiritual parent? Who in the Church has handed on the faith to you? Who in the Church has taught you about the Bible? Which family members? Which priests or deacons or bishops? Remember their teaching and thank God for them today.

DAY 5

Remember the wedding at Cana in John 2? Mary says to the servants the same thing she says to you and to me today: "Do whatever He tells you" (John 2:5). She will help us always look to Him. By being who she is, she teaches us about Jesus. And that's why we say, echoing the words of Gabriel in the Gospel of Luke, "Hail [Mary], full of grace, the Lord is with you!" (Luke 1:28). And that's why we ask her, with all of our hearts, "Please pray for us—we who are sinners—now and at the hour of our death. Amen."

† Open your Bible today. Read Luke 1:28, 42. This is the first half of the Hail Mary prayer. Ask Jesus to teach you the right way to see Mary today. Ask Him to teach you how to see her through Gabriel's eyes, Elizabeth's eyes, and His own eyes.

DAY 6

After Jesus was crucified, Mary lived in a city called Ephesus in what is now Turkey, alongside St. John the Apostle and Evangelist, who was bishop there, until the end of her days. In AD 431, all the bishops of the world—or most of them—gathered in Ephesus to talk about Jesus and the nature of His humanity and divinity. Places are important. It was fitting that debates about Jesus's nature would be held in the place where Mary and St. John had lived.

† Which places are important to your walk with Jesus? Maybe there's a place at your house or in your town where you've had profound encounters with God. Go back there soon, physically or in your imagination. Thank God for that experience. Rest in the grace of the past. Then ask Jesus if He has any deeper graces for you in the present.

DAY 7

At the Council of Ephesus, someone said that Jesus was really two persons—not one person with a human nature and a divine nature, but two persons in one body. The bishops, led by St. Cyril of Alexandria, said no. The Bible and the tradition of the Church teach us that Jesus is one person—fully God and fully man. And that means the mother whom He created for Himself can truly be called Mother of God. And that's why we honor Mary so deeply—because she bears God to us, because she brings God to us, because she points always to Jesus.

† The truth that Jesus is one divine person who has both a human and a divine nature is fundamental to our lives as Christians. And Mary, the Mother of God, surrounds, protects, and elucidates that truth. This is Mary's vocation: to mother, to protect, and to bear forth Jesus. Having been given as mother to all of Jesus's disciples at the foot of the cross (John 19:25–27), she also mothers us. Remembering that Jesus has given her to us as our mother, too, ask Mary for help in those places where you need help today.

WEEK 2
St. Basil & St. Gregory
Bishops and Doctors of the Church

Patron saints of education, exorcisms, liturgists, and monks, among others

FEAST DAY: January 2

DAY 1

We take our next step on our journey with our friends in heaven by turning toward two great saints who were friends on earth: St. Basil the Great and St. Gregory of Nazianzus. There's a saying that "saints come in pairs." When Jesus sent forth His disciples to prepare the way for His coming, He sent them "two by two" (Luke 10:1, Mark 6:7). They were able to lean on and support one another.

† Who is in your support network? Who can you lean on when things get tough and rejoice with when things are good? Who knows your struggles well enough to support you when you're down and to call you higher when you sin? If you don't have someone like this in your life, ask Jesus to bring a best friend into your life, and ask Basil and Gregory to pray for you.

DAY 2

Both Basil and Gregory were blessed with families devoted to goodness and holiness. Basil came from a family of saints, including his parents, Basil the Elder and Emmelia of Caesarea. His brothers and sisters—both those who were married and those who were consecrated to God—were all renowned for their piety. Basil's eldest sister, Macrina, and two of his brothers, Gregory of Nyssa and Peter of Sebaste, are also officially numbered among the saints. Gregory's parents are, too—his father, also named Gregory, and his mother, Nonna.

† Most of our families are not as saint-filled as these families, but most of our families do contain saintly examples. Who in your family is a holy example for you? Think of one of his or her virtues and put it into practice this week.

DAY 3

Both born and raised in the region of Cappadocia (in what is now Turkey), Basil and Gregory both found themselves in Athens for studies, where the spark of the acquaintance they'd made in Basil's hometown of Caesarea was fanned into a flame of deep friendship. Gregory himself said, "We had come, like streams of a river, from the same source in our native land, had separated from each other in pursuit of learning, and were now united again as if by plan, for God so arranged it."

† Who among your acquaintances might be able to become this kind of friend? Someone at church? At work? Talk to that person. Grab coffee together. See if there's potential for a deeper friendship.

DAY 4

The ancient philosopher Aristotle said that friendship can be based on utility, enjoyment, or virtue. Friendships based on utility are like business arrangements, while those based on enjoyment might include either wholesome diversions or sinful ones. Both are self-focused, depending on people's usefulness to each other or their enjoyment of their time together. Friendships based on virtue, on the other hand, are complete or perfect friendships, wherein two people focus on each other's good. Gregory wrote, "The same hope inspired us: the pursuit of learning. This is an ambition especially subject to envy. Yet between us there was no envy. On the contrary, we made capital out of our rivalry. Our rivalry consisted, not in seeking the first place for oneself but in yielding it to the other, for we each looked on the other's success as his own."

† Thank God today for the friends with whom you have virtuous friendships.

DAY 5

These days, the concept of intimacy between friends is nearly lost. But to Gregory and Basil, such pure and holy friendship was "that flame that was to bind us together . . . When, in the course of time, we acknowledged our friendship and recognized that our ambition was a life of true wisdom, we became everything to each other." Basil and Gregory were together in pursuit of learning, God, and virtue. Their brotherly love spurred each on to sainthood, a sanctity that often "comes in pairs."

† How do you normally respond to invitations into the intimacy of friendship? Can you talk to your friends (or at least a few of them) about the deep things of life? Your aspirations? Your goals? Your relationship with God?

DAY 6

Basil is sometimes called the "Father of Eastern Monasticism." Having spent time as a monk himself, he supervised monasteries of both men and women, even after becoming a bishop. His guidance for monks and nuns is still followed in many parts of the world today.

For Gregory's part, he taught St. Jerome, the great Bible scholar, and presided over the Council of Constantinople, which finalized the Nicene Creed we proclaim each Sunday at Mass. Their lives continue to influence the daily lives of all Christians today.

† How can you influence the lives of others? Can you give a bit of time to mentor someone personally?

DAY 7

On this final day of our reflections on the dear friends Basil and Gregory, let us allow ourselves to be mentored by the writings of Basil regarding something most of us struggle with: anger and unforgiveness. "Do not overturn your own purpose, and do not appear to be easily accessible to those who insult you," he wrote. "Let him bark at you ineffectually; let it burst upon himself. For the one who strikes one who feels no pain takes vengeance on himself, for neither is his enemy repaid, nor is his temper assuaged. Likewise, the person reproaching one unaffected by abuse is unable to find relief for his passion. On the contrary, as I have said, he is indeed cut to the heart."

† Basil puts our temptations to anger and unforgiveness into perspective. How can thinking with a different perspective change our day-to-day actions?

WEEK 3
St. Elizabeth Ann Seton
Religious sister and founder of the Sisters of Charity

Patron saint of Catholic schools, seafarers, widows, and the state of Maryland

FEAST DAY: January 4

DAY 1

On September 14, 1975, Pope St. Paul VI canonized Elizabeth Ann
Seton, officially declaring her a saint. "Canonize" is the verb we use to
say that someone has been officially declared to be a saint and added
to the "canon," or official listing of recognized saints of the Church.
A saint is any person in heaven or, even more broadly, anyone who
has received the gift of baptism (1 Corinthians 1:2). But what does
it take to be officially declared a saint? Two things: heroic virtue and
evidence of effective prayers after death. Every officially declared saint
has shown in his or her life some great virtue.

† Though you may not be called to canonization, you are called to be a
saint. That means that God has both destined and empowered you
and me, by the gift of baptism, to live with heroic virtue. What is one
virtue in which God might be calling you to grow right now?

DAY 2

As James 5:16 says, "the prayer of a righteous person has great power
in its effects." After a person who has shown heroic virtue dies, people
who knew the person will often begin to ask for prayers. The idea is:
If she was really close to God on earth, then she must be in heaven.
If she's in heaven, then she's even closer to God. So I'll keep asking

her to pray for me. By the time Elizabeth died, her life spoke clearly of her heroic virtue, and those who knew her began to ask her to pray for them from heaven. If this person's intercession is proven through two scientifically verified miracles, the saint is canonized, and his or her name is allowed to be used in liturgy—in public worship—as an intercessor before the throne of God.

† Do you know someone in your life, now passed away, who lived with heroic virtue? Say a prayer for that person, asking God in His mercy to bring him or her into heaven. Then ask him or her to pray for you: "_____, if you are in heaven with Jesus right now, please pray for me. Please ask Jesus our Lord to help me with _____."

DAY 3

Born in New York in 1774, Elizabeth was the first person from what is now the United States to be canonized. In his homily at her canonization, Pope St. Paul VI proclaimed, "St. Elizabeth Ann Seton is an American. All of us say this with spiritual joy, and with the intention of honoring the land and the nation from which she marvelously sprang forth as the first flower in the calendar of the saints . . . Rejoice, we say to the great nation of the United States of America. Rejoice for your glorious daughter."

† Every culture that has ever arisen has both great virtues and terrible vices. What is one virtue present in your culture that you'd like to cultivate in yourself? Perhaps it's one present in American ideals, such as hard work, freedom, or patriotism. How can you cultivate this virtue in your own life?

DAY 4

As a religious sister, Elizabeth served the poor of the United States. In such a prosperous land, she encountered the opposite of prosperity, and her heart was moved with the love of Jesus, who invited her to care for the "least of these" (Matthew 25:40). From this desire in her own heart—having been both rich and poor in her lifetime—Elizabeth began the Catholic school movement in America by offering the country's first free Catholic school, in Emmitsburg, Maryland.

† In a society marked by individualism, Elizabeth chose to practice the virtue of interdependent solidarity—what Pope St. John Paul II called "a firm and persevering determination to commit oneself to the common good. That is to say to the good of all and of each individual, because we are all really responsible for all." Let us imitate Elizabeth in the practice of this important virtue of solidarity. We could do so by spending time with those who are lonely, providing for the needs of the poor, or using our knowledge to help those who struggle in school.

DAY 5

In a saint's life, we're sure to find suffering. If, as Mother Teresa said, "suffering[s] are but the kiss of Jesus," then we shouldn't be surprised when the saints receive many such kisses. Jesus suffered much, and He gives us the gift of being like Him in our sufferings. One such suffering in the life of Elizabeth was her husband William's tuberculosis. During perilous economic times, the stress on William worsened this disease, so he, Elizabeth, and their eldest daughter traveled to Italy in hopes that the Italian climate would bolster his health. However, William died in Italy shortly after their arrival.

† Thank Jesus for one kiss you have received from Him recently in the form of suffering. Ask Him to use this to help you become a saint (whether you're ever canonized or not).

DAY 6

Stranded in Italy after her husband's death, Elizabeth and her daughter Anna Maria were taken in by her late husband's Italian business partners. The great charity of the devout Filicchi family provided a vibrant example of Catholic life that greatly attracted Elizabeth, who had been raised Anglican. Struggling with the movements in her heart and mind to convert to Catholicism, she prayed a portion of "The Universal Prayer" by Alexander Pope: "If I am right, Thy grace impart, still in the right to stay; If I am wrong, O, teach my heart to find that better way." With sincere prayer as well as fasting, Elizabeth became Catholic on Ash Wednesday, 1805, and received her first Communion on March 25.

† Thank God today for someone who has shown you the love of Jesus, especially when you were down and out, as the Filicchi family did for Elizabeth.

DAY 7

Converting to Catholicism in the early 1800s in New York was a socially momentous move. Elizabeth knew that, with this decision, she would lose much support and economic opportunity. Yet she made the courageous decision to follow her conscience, which had been convicted of the truth that the Church Jesus founded (Matthew 16:18–20) truly subsists in the Catholic Church and nowhere else.

† Convert or not—Catholic or not—we will each face persecution if we are serious about living the gospel (Matthew 10:24–25). Where can you follow Elizabeth's example of courage? Do you need to stand up more for those who are being gossiped about? Do you need to study more about your faith to respond to challenges from others? How can you be courageous in living and spreading the faith that has been gifted to you?